SOUTH DAKOTA DAYS

Frank Lyons

South Dakota Days is based entirely on Frank Lyons's memory of his youth in South Dakota in the 1930s and 1940s.

Front book cover picture, *The Prairie Is My Garden*—Harvey Dunn.
Back book cover photograph, *Dakota Sunrise*—Nona Lyons.

The author may be contacted at:
fwlyons4@mchsi.com or (309) 788-7983.

ISBN-13: 978-1466424425
ISBN-10: 1466424427

Dedicated to the memory of the author's parents,
Bill and Mary (Donohoe) Lyons.

And with gratitude to my friend, Bob Chaney, for
the use of his beach house while writing
these stories in Akumal, Mexico.

CONTENTS

Introduction	vii
Chapter 1 ♦ The Great Depression	1
Chapter 2 ♦ Country Roads	9
Chapter 3 ♦ Water	14
Chapter 4 ♦ Cattle Culture	19
Chapter 5 ♦ Country Dances	26
Chapter 6 ♦ The Gunnery Range	31
Chapter 7 ♦ Doing the Chores	37
Chapter 8 ♦ The Day They Turned on the Juice	44
Chapter 9 ♦ The Day the New Tractor Came	49
Chapter 10 ♦ The Day the Cow Danced on Me	54
Chapter 11 ♦ Domestic Life on the Farm	60
Chapter 12 ♦ Things to Make Life Better on the Farm	73
Chapter 13 ♦ The Neighbors	82
Chapter 14 ♦ The Threshers	97
Chapter 15 ♦ My Aunts	107
Chapter 16 ♦ My Uncles	116
Chapter 17 ♦ Where There's Boredom, There's Hope	129
Chapter 18 ♦ The Day the Draft Letter Came	141
Final Thoughts	149

INTRODUCTION

My roots extend deep into the rich soil of the farm where I was born and raised in the Missouri and James River valleys of Yankton County, South Dakota. My ethnic roots extend far deeper into the faraway, misty crevasses of Irish history in County Waterford and County Westmeath, the ancestral homes of my forebears—the Lyons and Donohoe families.

My outlook on life was firmly and unalterably set by the people and events that I knew in the 1930s and 1940s within a small semi-circle centered at our farm. The flat segment of the semi-circle was the Missouri River that marked the border between South Dakota and Nebraska.

My outlook could not have been more firmly and indelibly imbedded in my psyche if it had been chiseled on a marble tablet. There were never any doubts on matters of right or wrong; ethics; spirituality; tolerance for all creeds, races, and customs; sympathy for the underdog; steadfast commitment to family, friends, and colleagues; and the proper regard for wealth and material possessions.

These principles became the touchstones for the rest of my life. They come close to Thomas Jefferson's when he wrote in The United States Declaration of Independence, "We hold these truths to be self evident..."

A serious examination of my life in regard to adherence to these lofty and noble principles would likely show an occasional wobble to the right or left of true north, but when this happened it was always with a firm voice whispering in my ear that a detour was underway.

The stories in this book are based on my memories of events from far off times. Some may have accumulated a coat of gilt when in reality the originals were brushed with common barn paint. Others may be like a string-tied file of disorganized papers, faded pictures, and yellow clippings retrieved from a forgotten cubby hole. It's even possible that a few of the remembered events never happened. If the stories are amusing, but in some instances receive low marks when subjected to fact-checks, I propose that the reader kindly let them stand.

The stories recall, record, and share cherished memories from a distant age that was crammed with wonder, excitement, expectation, discovery, and dreams.

CHAPTER ONE

THE GREAT DEPRESSION

*...and the wheat blowed out and the hard-working people just stumbling about,
bothered with mortgages, debts, bills, sickness,
worries of everything blowing kind,
I seen there was plenty to make up songs about...*
—Woodie Guthrie

The Great Depression was the dominant event of the 1930s in the U.S. and much of the world. The economy was throttled. Unemployment reached as high as thirty-three percent. Families were in dire straits. The Midwest received a "triple whammy" when the Great Depression teamed up with searing drought, grasshopper hordes, and dust storms.

Long gone was the extravagant 1869 vision of the southeastern Dakota Territory noted in an historical article. The article reports the claims of a promoter of Yankton County:

> In the exuberance of his fancy, this transplanted Cork man (Irish promoter) arrayed his newly acquired lands in the apparel of romance, clothing them with beautiful groves, waving grain fields, and brilliant gardens.

The Great Depression overwhelmingly influenced the lives of my parents, Bill and Mary Lyons, as it did most Americans.

It was not just a time for belt tightening and waiting for good times to return; it was a time of misery, hunger, deprivation, hopelessness, and erosion of confidence in the free enterprise system. It was a time when much of the economy shut down and businesses turned employees out into the streets. It was a time of bank failures with their customers deprived of every dime they possessed. It was a time of foreclosures on home, farm, and ranch mortgages. Safety nets such as the Federal Deposit Insurance Corporation (FDIC) did not yet exist.

For many, it was such a devastating psychological experience that they could not cope. It was not uncommon for parents to abandon their families, commit suicide, or go into deep psychological depressions. The long duration of the Great Depression made it a way of life for a generation of people. Even after it ended, some people were too traumatized to ever resume normal lives.

Some Americans thought Russia, since its 1917 revolution and brutal conversion to communism, had developed a workable, utopian structure for providing equitable social, economic, and political systems. They believed that because the capitalistic system of the US was faltering, it should be abandoned and replaced with Russian communism. Lincoln Steffens, upon returning from a "sanitized and controlled" trip to Russia said, "I have been over in the future—and it works!"

Early in the depression, the administration of President Herbert Hoover could not come to grips with the country's rapidly collapsing economic and social institutions. There was no model to follow for a debacle of such magnitude. The federal government was paralyzed. The country was in despair. Washington could only recite platitudes such as, "Prosperity is just around the corner."

In early 1933, Franklin Delano Roosevelt became the president of the U.S. His administration took immediate "tree shaking" action to try to restore the country's collapsing economic and social systems.

He gave the country hope with his jaunty, confident presence in the White House. He understood how to communicate with the American people with his frequent "fireside radio chats" broadcast from his ancestral home on the Hudson River. The measured tones of his cultured and confident voice and his hopeful messages made most people feel that their government was now in capable hands.

Hungry, Homeless, and Helpless

However, President Roosevelt traveled a road strewn with obstacles. Entrenched status quo politicians and citizens built roadblocks to stymie his aggressive recovery programs; they saw them as socialistic, radical, and a betrayer of the established principles of self-reliance upon which the country was built.

Bread Line
—Franklin D. Roosevelt Museum

Roosevelt's new programs started to provide aid for the dire needs of the people, but final relief from the Great Depression did not come until the late 1930s and early 1940s with the start of World War II.

In spite of severe economic difficulties, my parents hung on to their farm. Millions of farmers and ranchers in the country were less fortunate.

My paternal grandparents, who could not pay their bank loan of $1,600 to the Federal Land Bank, lost their farm. They never recovered; they lived the rest of their lives dependent on their children.

The Civilian Conservation Corps (CCC) was one of President Roosevelt's "alphabet soup" relief programs designed to invigorate the economy. My Uncle Bob signed up for the CCC. For his work building roads and parks in the Black Hills, he earned thirty dollars per month.

Great Depression Farm Auction
A Day of Despair

The paymaster sent twenty-five dollars to his desperate parents. This remittance was their only income. Some in the CCC started to receive square meals and live in secure, comfortable quarters for the first time in many years.

Many wealthy people, who were insulated from the Great Depression, shielded their wealth from public view. They stopped buying custom-bodied Duisenbergs and V-12 Pierce-Arrows in favor of boxy Buicks and stodgy Chryslers. The luxury automobile industry in the U.S. folded up. The excesses of the wealthy, as disclosed in F. Scott Fitzgerald's *The Great Gatsby,* were over until a later generation. Being wealthy was not as much fun if it could not be publicly flouted.

During the Great Depression, life was especially hard on young people. Many were deprived of a college education. But if there was enough determination, a way could sometimes be found.

My cousin James arrived at our farmhouse door in the mid-1930s. He had driven twenty-five cattle a hundred miles from his father's ranch to market and sold them for a few dollars; worked for a farmer until he "dried out" (crops burned up from the drought); and hitchhiked and walked another sixty miles to our farm. James had a cheerful, indomitable spirit. My father and an uncle hired him as a farmhand for seventy-five cents per day. They tucked his wages away in a jar. At the end of the summer, James went to a nearby teacher's college where he placed his money on the registrar's table and said, "I want to register for college; this is all I have." The registrar took the money and found him a job so he could enroll. Although the depression broke the spirit of some people, it toughened up my cousin; no problem in his long life was ever again insurmountable.

Uncle Dennis Lyons, James's father, was a pioneer settler in Tripp County on the South Dakota prairies. In 1910, at the age of twenty-one, he drove to Tripp County with his sixteen-year-old bride, Bessie, and three horse-drawn freight wagons. For $1,600 and a $6 donation to an Indian welfare fund, Uncle Dennis bought a "relinquishment" and, with high hopes for a prosperous future, started his adult life as a rancher. A "relinquishment" resulted when the original homesteader abandoned his claim to the land.

In 1933, Uncle Dennis poignantly wrote—with a little help from H. W. Longfellow and E. A. Allen—about the Great Depression in his county:

Dust Storm

Finally in the ever-onward march of time, I find myself almost to the quarter century point of development of this county. I live with the dreams of twenty-five years vanished, with fancy's pictures faded, with youth gone, and age here; with economic disaster spreading despair in its wake, and with drought and grasshoppers making the land uninhabitable. But from the human heart springs hope eternal, and in the active hours of daylight with sober logic born of experience, I can again see a future, as I know history has always repeated itself. But in the evening between the daylight and darkness, when comes the pause in life's occupations a still voice whispers to me, Backward turn backward, Oh time in your flight.

Uncle Dennis lived for many years in desperate economic circumstances that did not allow him to fully develop his considerable intellectual talent. His plight could be described with a slightly adjusted line from a poem by Thomas Gray: "Full many a flower is born to blush unseen and waste its sweetness on the prairie air."

Farmers and ranchers had an edge over urban families; many could hold out for longer periods of time by growing their own food and fuel and "making do" for most of their other needs while they waited for good times to return.

The chorus of *Dakota Land* sums up the terrible drought:

Oh Dakota Land, sweet Dakota land,
As on thy burning soil I stand,
I look across the plains,
And wonder why it never rains.

Even though the Great Depression surrounded my parents like a pall, they shielded their children from stress and hardship. For us, growing up on our farm during the Great Depression was a happy, easygoing experience. Life was secure, happy, and normal.

CHAPTER TWO

COUNTRY ROADS

I'm forty miles of bad road,
A riverbed of pot holes

—Duane Eddy

In South Dakota in the 1930s, good roads were largely confined to the imagination of mapmakers. Our farm road was a rutted dirt track between two barb wire fences. It ended a half mile to the south where it intersected with Highway 50, a two lane gravel road. The highway ran three miles west to Yankton and sixty miles east to Sioux City, Iowa.

In the spring, as the frost went out of the ground, the dirt road became a bottomless quagmire of soupy mud.

When my mother drove to town for her weekly Saturday grocery shopping, my father towed her in our 1928 Dodge sedan to the gravel road with a team of horses; he would return at an agreed upon time to tow her back home. He sat on the car fender while driving the team. Horse hooves had better traction in the mud than spinning tires.

In the winter when snow drifts blocked the roads, farmers could be holed up at home for weeks. In emergencies, horse-drawn sleds, foot power, or saddle horses were the only means for seeking help.

Washing and shining rural cars was a futile effort; several yards of travel stirred up sky-high clouds of dust. Dust clung to cars as if attracted by an electrical charge and mud bonded to every surface like a coat of thick paint. Rural cars and trucks were easy to identify by their crust of dust and mud. Good observers could tell which area they came from by the color and texture of the dirt.

Dirt Road

Rural bridges were often in no better condition than the roads. While driving a team of horses to my grandparents' farm, I came to a wooden bridge across a trickle of a creek a half mile west of our farm. A truck's dual rear wheels had broken through the rotting bridge planking. It took a day of jacking and prying to raise the truck and re-plank the bridge.

Western roads were defined on early land maps as mandated by the Homestead Act of 1862. The act called for road rights-of-way to surround each section of land (one square mile.) Roads shown on the maps were often only barb wire fences or rarely used paths.

Roads were vital to farmers and ranchers for transporting animals, grain, and hay to markets. When it was time to market livestock, delays due to bad roads could be costly.

In the 1920s and 1930s, political pressure for road funding grew rapidly. Motorists demanded better roads as the sale of cars sky-rocketed; farmers clamored for better roads for hauling their products to market.

In the mid-1930s, funding was appropriated for road improvement in our county. Earth-moving machines came to work the dirt road in front of our farm; they graded a crown on the road center to shed water and ditches to hold rain run-off. In a few more years the road surface was graveled. For the next seventy-five years, the road would remain unchanged.

Road-building brought a brief cash windfall to my father. It was the depth of the depression and cash was virtually non-existent. My father earned five dollars a day for several weeks for himself, a horse team, and a Fresno—a flat bladed earth scraper—to build driveways from the new roads to farmsteads and fields. Skilled horsemanship was required to prevent damaging the galvanized culverts installed under each driveway.

Farmers had the informal "pasturing rights" for the road ditches by their farms. Our tedious job as boys was to herd our five milk cows in the ditches so they could graze for a couple hours each morning and afternoon. In remoter areas, the roads were grown over with weeds and grass except for a pair of ruts left by an occasional passing car, truck, or wagon. This added to the area available for free pasturing.

When cars drove by on sparsely-used country roads as farmers worked in their fields near the road, it was essential that they stop for a talk. Car or tractor engines were always left running no matter how long the talks lasted. Even though work might be pressing, conversations were never hastened.

Road Grading with Fresno

Roadside communications that were crystal clear to farmers were a challenge for outsiders to understand:

> Are you going to the State Fair this year?
> Garsh, the misses was just talking about it the other day
>   (The answer is yes.)
> I'll be needing some help next week to haul hay; can I use
>   your hired hand?
> Waall, he complained about a sore wrist when he finished
>   shucking corn yesterday. (The answer is no.)

Are you planning to sign up for the new Fire Protection
Association?
By golly, it sure looks like the corn prices are going to stay
low again this fall. (The answer is no.)

Country road conversations were about livestock, grain, and hay
prices—too low if selling and too high if buying; livestock diseases and
deaths; weather; Saturday night misbehavior of the neighbors or hired
men; accidents and misfortunes; the best farm equipment; crop yields;
trucks; hunting; dogs; farm loan interest rates; planting and harvest plans;
and the voting record of the dopes and dummies running the government in Washington.

County road traffic was sparse; when a cloud of dust was visible or
engine noise audible, people turned to the road to see who was driving by
and to report on it at the next meal. If a stranger passed, speculation and
curiosity ran high. Rural neighborhoods had the "eyes of the jungle."

The magnificent all-season paved roads and interstate highways of
the future would be far faster and safer for whisking strangers and goods
to distant places. But the impersonal travelers would have no more
knowledge of the lives of the people on wayside farms, ranches, and
villages than if they zipped past in tunnels under the fields or soared
above the clouds.

Although country roads were less traveled, they conveyed some of
the most genuine people in the world with their dreams, burdens of
sorrow, hopes for prosperity, and acceptance of their place in the scheme
of life.

CHAPTER THREE

WATER

And souls that cry for water
Clear, cool, water.

—Marty Robbins

On our Missouri and James River bottoms farm, we were blessed with easy access to potable water—unlike so many other farmers and ranchers who struggled to find a reliable supply of pure water.

A sand point well could be easily hammered into the sandy soil of our farm to the water table twenty feet below the surface. The sand point was a one and half-inch diameter, three foot long, pointed pipe with perforations covered with fine bronze screening to sift out sand. As the sand point was pounded into the sandy soil, additional lengths of pipe were screwed onto it until it reached a depth of thirty feet. A cast iron, hand-operated pump was added to complete the well. We had a sand point well in our basement to supply water to the kitchen sink and another well in the hog house. Farmers could easily drive their own sand point wells.

An artesian well in our barnyard, supplied a copious amount of free-flowing water into cattle and horse water tanks. The water was warm and heavily laden with minerals. It came from an aquifer several hundred feet deep. The aquifer pressurized the water; no pumping was needed. The water overflowed the animal tanks and drained into a four-hundred foot long, sandy bottom pond that dissipated the excess water.

Professional well drillers built artesian wells. The community driller was "Swede Al." He had a long flowing white beard that gave him the appearance of a biblical prophet wearing rubber boots, bib overalls, and a plaid cap with earflaps.

The voluminous supply of artesian water made it a miniature spa. The large livestock tanks were a place for boys to have water fights on hot days, to store and cool ripe watermelons, and for cattle and horses to slake their enormous thirsts. In winter, a tall plume of water vapor rose from the artesian water pond and could be seen from a mile away.

The artesian well also supplied water for a summer makeshift shower—a bucket with holes punched in the bottom. The water temperature was raised further by storing it all day in a fifty-five gallon steel barrel in the hot sun.

On farms without artesian water, the wells were usually powered by windmills on top of twenty foot high wooden towers. The windmills had broad tails that turned the rotating blades into the wind. The tails also told the direction of the wind. The wind direction and speed of the mill blade rotation helped farmers and ranchers determine the likelihood of rain or storms.

In winter, the family took Saturday night baths in a white, cast iron bathtub with water heated on the kitchen range. When the tub was filled with as many boys as would fit in, it became a place for water sport.

The hired farm hands took their weekly baths in town in the rear of barber shops before they made their rounds to the pool hall, bowling alley, saloons, card joints, and possibly the second floor apartments on Broadway where "soiled doves" offered adult entertainment. The farm hands paid twenty cents for a bath, soap, towel, and a shake of talcum powder.

In winter there was always soft water for hair washing and delicate clothes laundering in the kitchen range reservoir. The water came from snow hauled into the kitchen in bushel baskets and dumped into the heated reservoir.

At my grandparents' house sixty miles to the west, potable water was not available from their windmill-powered well. It was too alkaline for human consumption. They drove daily to a neighboring farm with good drinking water and hauled it home in five gallon milk cans. As a

General Purpose Livestock Watertank

small boy, it was fun to ride in their Model-A Ford for the water because of the excitement when we forded Choteau Creek on the way to the neighbor's well. In the summer when ponds dried up in the sun, they were ringed with white alkaline powder. Farm animals had better digestive systems than humans; they could drink the alkaline water.

My grandparents used their cistern to cool milk and butter in summer months. They placed the food in a bucket and lowered it with a rope into the cool water.

There was another use for the water from the Missouri and James Rivers. In winter, farmers sawed ice into hundred pound blocks for storage in ice houses. Sawing ice on the frozen rivers was a dangerous job; the ice handlers could easily slip into the freezing open water.

Windmill Pumping Water

Ice houses were wooden structures, typically fifteen feet square. The ice blocks were buried in layers of insulating sawdust. Most of the ice remained frozen through the summer. Its principle use was to cool iceboxes for food storage. It was also used in hand-cranked ice cream makers, a special treat for summer picnics, birthdays, and Fourth of July celebrations.

When farmers went to the fields, they took drinking water with them in half-gallon Mason jars. They wrapped the jars with multiple layers of wet burlap sacking held in place with binder twine or bailing wire. Evaporation cooled the water. In times of heavy-duty farm work such as haying or threshing, farmers also hauled water to the fields in barrels for the horses.

Discharge water from the kitchen sink and bath water drained through four inch clay tiles to an open cesspool located in the sandy soil about three-hundred feet from the back of our house. The cesspool was ten feet in diameter.

In summer, a concrete-lined cistern stored soft rainwater collected from the house roof. The cistern was eight feet in diameter and twenty feet deep. Soft water has a silky feeling compared to the harsher feeling of mineral-laden well water.

Farmers and ranchers usually drank water from a community dipper or tin cup hung on a hook by the farmyard wells. It was a challenge to select the section of the dipper edge "least contaminated" by the mouths of previous drinkers. A popular newspaper cartoon showed a farmer awkwardly drinking from the "far side" of the dipper. Unknown to him, everyone else also drank from the same side.

CHAPTER FOUR

CATTLE CULTURE

*In Africa, cattle have been around for 9,000 years. The ancient
Maasai tribes of Kenya and Tanzania measure a man's success
by the number of his cattle and his children.*

Just after dinner time, attendance was usually good at the livestock
sales ring at the east city limits of Yankton, South Dakota. The ring was
little different from the Roman arenas that dominated Europe and
Northern Africa more than two thousand years earlier. The seats formed
a semi-circle around a fenced ring with straw on the floor. Gates on each
side allowed livestock to enter—similar to the Roman Coliseum except
there were no exotic animals from distant lands. Whereas the Roman
arenas were made by slaves from finished marble, the Yankton arena was
made by stockyard hands from rough-sawn lumber.

The sales arena had the atmosphere of a farmers and ranchers men's
club; some came from several hundred miles for the sales. A few came to
loiter in a warm, convivial place while their wives did their weekly
shopping and catching up on community news.

Selling was directed by the hypnotic chant of a glib auctioneer. He
needed to convince the sellers he was getting the highest price for their
cattle and other animals while simultaneously convincing the buyers he
offered a good deal for them. He called as many potential buyers by
name as he could remember over the loudspeaker in a tone indicating
each was his best friend. To give the buyers time to consider raising their
bids, the auctioneer bantered about anything that came to his mind and
extolled the qualities of the animals in the ring. He also hinted it was a
good time to buy due to the favorable economic outlook that he foresaw.

Several cane-waving assistants with the eyes of hawks faced potential buyers sitting on the benches. The buyers had guarded ways of bidding—a flick of a finger, a lifted eyebrow, or a slight nod. Apparently, if a buyer gave a bid noticeable to other buyers, he was regarded as a bit of a showoff.

A meticulous clerk sat on a chair on the stage to record the sales details so his sales slips could be used later when it was "settling up" time.

Usually, a brand inspector was at hand with a hair clipper in his pocket. His job was to shear the cattle enough to reveal their brands and assure buyers that the cattle had not been rustled.

Most of the cattle sold were calves weighing 500 pounds or yearlings at 750 pounds. They normally came from western ranches where they were grass fed since birth. The buyers, such as my father, bought cattle and fed them corn, silage, and hay until mid summer when they grew to 1200 pounds, the ideal size for market and slaughter. My father had a strong preference for Hereford cattle—commonly called White Faces. By market time, he would know each animal individually. Typically he bought 125 cattle each fall to grow and fatten in his feedlots four miles east of town.

Truckers also sat in the sales ring; the engines of their slat-sided semis idling outside until animal buyers hired them to haul newly purchased cattle to their farm feedlots. It was normally after dark when the frightened and miserable animals were driven, with urging by electric prods, into the trucks for the trip to their new homes. Confinement was difficult for cattle after living in the freedom of the open ranges; on the other hand, feed lot eating would be tastier than grass, and the sheltered living would be better.

The livestock sales ring was operated by Nis and Hans Calleson, a pair of immigrant Danish farmers. After a good business transaction, they sometimes celebrated with my father by drinking a few swigs of bourbon in their makeshift office under the sales ring seats.

The Calleson brothers were tireless; after closing the sale in Yankton in the late evening, one of them would stretch out in the back seat of a late model Nash sedan and have a stockyard hand drive him four hundred miles west to another sales ring in Rapid City. At dawn he would be rested and ready to participate in another cattle sale where he bought calves and yearlings to truck to their Yankton sales yard.

The Calleson brothers enjoyed summer trips home to Denmark during the low time of the cattle sales business. Travel was mostly by ship. They usually took a new Nash car with them to drive when they arrived in Denmark.

The Calleson brothers were my father's friends. He depended on them for their judgment of livestock quality and price. Sometimes he gave them authority to acquire cattle for him sight unseen.

When it was time to sell fattened cattle, they were trucked to the holding yards of the major meat packing centers in Sioux City, Sioux Falls, Omaha, and Kansas City. Surrounding the maze of plank-fenced pens in the sales yards stood the imposing multi-story meat packing plants of Cudahy, Armour, Swift, and John Morrell. The link between the stock yards and the packing plants was a multitude of livestock commission firms. Commission firms provided the pens and the liaison with the packing plant buyers who imperiously rode horse-back through the yards while they astutely sized up the cattle and price trends. The commission men negotiated with the packing house buyers to settle on the highest price possible for client's cattle.

The daily livestock market report from Sioux City was always given over radio station WNAX—570 on the dial—by a folksy announcer named Don Cunningham. He called old cows "Shelly Nellies"; a dull market was "like kissing your sister." Woe onto people at farm and ranch dinner tables who talked when the livestock market reports were being broadcast. Cunningham always signed off by enigmatically saying, "Goodbye, Fitz."

My father used Swanson, Gilmore, and Carroll as his cattle commission firm. Charlie Carroll was their representative in our community. Charlie, dressed in his trade mark white Stetson hat, boots, and western gabardine clothes, was a colorful man. When he came to the Yankton

Bill Lyons and Leonard Holzbauer
at Sioux City Cattle Sale

area to call on his clients and assess their cattle, he stayed overnight at our farm. He and my father stayed up past midnight talking at the kitchen table over a fresh bottle of whiskey. Charlie did most of the talking with his long colorful tales and sipped most of the whiskey. The next morning, my mother always filled the empty whiskey bottle with cold coffee for Charlie's consumption later in the morning.

During the summer, I drove Charlie's new white Fords for him on his visits to community clients. In the evening Charlie returned to our house for the second night. He told my father about each call made during the day. The calls were all business-like, but when Charlie recounted the day's visits to my father, each was worthy of a routine for a stand-up comic. He characterized each farmer, his wife, his children, his dog, his cats, his horses, and his cattle in a hilarious light that was only visible to him.

My father usually visited the Sioux City livestock yards to witness his cattle sales. My mother and several of my siblings often accompanied him to Sioux City to shop. The price received for the cattle largely determined the family's annual income and prosperity. If the price was good, large purchases were often made such as new suits, a radio, or a major kitchen appliance. The market day's ritual included renting a room at Martin's Hotel where my grandmother, if she came along, could rest. My father would meet up with the family at the hotel after his day at the livestock yards.

When government-imposed price controls of World War II lifted, livestock prices immediately spiked. A new, green 1948 Plymouth sedan soon occupied our garage—the first new car my parents ever owned. It was almost as exciting as the day the first new tractor come to our farm.

Midwest cattle traditions continue to evolve from nine thousand year earlier when cattle were first domesticated. For centuries, they have provided milk to drink; meat to eat, tallow for candles; hooves for making gelatin; hides for manufacturing shoes, gloves, jackets, saddles, and harnesses; muscle power to pull heavy loads, and in later times, ingredients for making Elmer's glue. Cattle offer temporary respite from the cold when hugged by freezing farmers and cowboys, currency to buy brides, bragging rights for bumptious Texans, currency for trade, and inspiration for countless cowboy songs and movies. For centuries they have been one of the mainstays for the agoras of ancient Greece, the forums of Rome, the fairs of Ireland, and the animal markets of Africa.

Gentle, patient, and noble cattle have evolved into innumerable breeds to fit most climates and living conditions and developed to serve the many needs of man. In the Minoan culture of ancient Crete and in the modern Hindu faith of India, they were venerated. In the U.S., cattle are honored each year at state fairs, shows, roundups, jamborees, palavers, and festivals.

Grazing Hereford Cattle

Plodding cows, although careless with their personal modesty, are supreme in terms of dignity and serenity. They have their day in the sun at the annual National Cattle Congress in Waterloo, Iowa—big doings supplemented with a spelling bee, a tractor pull, and The Biggest Bull contest.

The cattle culture of the world continues to be as pervasive as it has been for thousands of years. On cloudless nights, those with keen vision and poetry in their souls can glimpse an agile bossy jumping over the moon. Those with acute hearing can hear the leathery voice of Vaughn Monroe singing his mournful 1950s song about red-eyed, steel-hoofed cattle thundering up dusty draws in the sky pursued by condemned cowboys for all eternity as punishment for their sinful lives on earth.

CHAPTER FIVE

COUNTRY DANCES

Come, let me sing into your ear,
Those dancing days are gone...
...I carry the sun in a golden cup
The moon in a silver bag.
—William Butler Yeats

In earlier and happier times, the Sioux Indians—also known as Lakota or Dakota—performed their Sun Dance with music to communicate with the Great Spirits and to re-instill a sense of tribal unity and identity as warriors. In later times, they despairingly hoped their Ghost Dance would bring back the bison and their dead warriors and grant victory over the white invaders who were destroying their culture.

Hordes of pioneers in wagon trains, on horseback, and on foot came west to claim plentiful open land—ignoring its occupancy by the ill-fated Sioux. The pioneers continued dancing on the prairie but according to their own music and dance traditions as they sawed out tunes on fiddles and danced any where there was a hard surface to stomp on.

As a fifteen year old boy in the mid 1940s, I "discovered" music and dancing even though they had been around for a long time. For several summers I worked as a farmhand on my Uncle Tom's farm in Charles Mix County, South Dakota. When weekend dances were scheduled in country dancehalls, the news spread faster than good gossip. Any dance within a radius of thirty miles was fair game. Uncle Tom generously loaned me his road-weary Ford sedan to drive the dusty dirt and gravel roads to the dances.

Country Dancing

Country dances were usually held in simple wooden buildings standing alone at rural crossroads. The landmark buildings also served as polling places, community meeting halls, churches, and schools. Most were not electrified.

The musicians, who performed without the benefit of electric amplification, were farmers, ranchers, merchants, clerks, students, and teachers. They played accordions, fiddles, guitars, banjos, clarinets, horns, and harmonicas. Clarence Cowman did not allow his missing arm to be a

Willowdale Ramblers
Country Dance Band
(Arlys and Mary Ellen Magorian; Jack, Betty, Tom,
and Bob Lyons; and Delores Remington)

handicap for playing the harmonica in his lively and popular Hayshaker Band.

Dancehall admission fare ranged from free to twenty-five cents for an inked stamp on the wrist.

The sound of waltzes, polkas, fox trots, and square dances extended far from open dancehall doors into the adjacent corn fields. The bands could be counted on to play "Comin' Around the Mountain," "My Old

Kentucky Home," "Home on the Range," "Tennessee Waltz," "McNamara's Band," and "Over the Rainbow."

The weekly Hit Parade, the ten most popular songs heard on radio, was the rage throughout the country and the source of the latest songs; all would soon to be heard in even the remotest dancehalls. Some of the songs making the Hit Parade list were: "Blue Berry Hill," "Pistol Packin' Mama," "Peg O' My Heart," and "When the Swallows Come Back to Capistrano."

World War II was in full swing. Patriotic songs struck an emotional note with most people when they thought of their friends and relatives away in the military—often fighting in combat: "The White Cliffs of Dover," "Boogie Woogie Bugle Boy," "Comin' in on a Wing and a Prayer," and "When the Lights Come on Again."

Big Band music and the Swing Era were "in." The bands of Benny Goodman, Duke Ellington, Glenn Miller, and Guy Lombardo were known to everyone—unless they lived in caves. Country bands played their songs even though they could not duplicate their sounds.

Teenagers, courting couples, young married couples, and older couples attended country dances. A few "bruisers" also came to dances to get soused and to pick fights.

Later in the evening, the sheriff might show up to check out the "temperature" of the doings and ensure that the fighters confined damage to bruises and cuts. They were often too far gone with whiskey to do much more than harmlessly paw at each other.

If dances were to celebrate weddings, money was "carefully" pinned to the bride's dress. A wedding invitation was not required for dancehall admittance.

Most teenagers did not come to dancehalls for the music or the dancing. They were discovering and trying to understand their chromosomes and hormones and learning the social skills required for interacting with the opposite gender.

The boys drew on all of their courage for the excruciatingly difficult task of asking girls to dance. Then they had to decide how close they could hold them to their agitated bodies. A bottle of beer sometimes facilitated matters.

The girls tried, without much success, to talk nonchalantly to their friends and pretend not to notice if they had to sit out dances.

If all went well on the dance floor, there might be an intermission sit-out period in the back seat of one of the parked Model-A Fords. And if luck ran especially good, a few chaste hugs and kisses might transpire.

As I recall this time in my teenage years so long ago, I remember my addled thoughts on the midnight drives back to Uncle Tom's farm after the musicians played "Home Sweet Home," the traditional final song of the evening:

> Did I say the right thing to the girls I danced with. Will I ever see any of them again? What's a boy–girl relationship really supposed to be all about? How did I look to the girls I met? Why did I act like such a clod? I wish I didn't get a dry mouth and blush when I talk to girls. It's sure a lot easier to talk to guys. Why can't I act like that hotshot football player who all the girls swoon over? But, who knows—maybe I did alright after all. None of the girls refused to dance with me. Maybe there is some hope that I will not act like such a dope around girls next time. I sure hope there'll be another dance somewhere next weekend.

Popular movies often starred dancers: Fred Astaire in tails, top hat, and patent leather dancing slippers and Ginger Rogers in chiffon gowns, glowing blond hair, and stiletto heels. As they swirled across the polished floor of elegant Hollywood ballrooms, they could not have enjoyed it more than I in my Montgomery Ward shirt and my partner in a home-made cotton dress as we sashayed across the pine floors of country dancehalls.

CHAPTER SIX

THE GUNNERY RANGE

When I died, they washed me out of my turret with a hose.
(The Death of the Ball Turret Gunner)
—Randall Jarrell

I was on my knees on the living room floor, beside my brothers, reading the comics (Superman, Red Ryder, and Orphan Annie) in the local *Press and Dakotan* newspaper when a mysterious, rumbling roar approached; it shook our farmhouse and rattled the dishes in the cupboard. We had never heard such a strange racket before. Roly, our dog, feared thunder; he cowered under a chair. We guessed it was an airplane because the noise pitch rapidly changed as if a train was approaching.

We ran outside and looked up as an awesome formation of Boeing four-engine B-17 Flying Fortresses thundered over our house. They seemed to be flying at silo-top elevation. The bristling gun turrets—tail, nose, belly, top, and sides—were visible. It was an astounding and unbelievable sight. The formation contained a dozen planes.

As the planes flew beyond our vision, we heard the faint stuttering of their machine guns as they neared the newly-built gunnery range seven miles west of our farm.

We soon learned that these B-17s were the vanguard for endless formations on training flights.

Until then, our only experience with aviation was the occasional sight of a single-engine Piper Cub plane. We knew World War II was going on, but for us it was a thing that was happening someplace else to other people. It did not touch our daily lives.

Boeing B-17 Flying Fortress

Our farm was sixty miles up the Missouri River from Sioux City, Iowa. It was 1942. I was twelve years old.

Industrial and military mobilization for the war was shifting into high gear at lightning speed. The country was undergoing the most massive economic and organizational transformation in history.

If we had read more than the comics in the newspapers, we might have known that seven miles south of Sioux City, a major Army Air Force training center for heavy bombers was being built and organized. On the other hand, with severe war time government censorship, it is possible that only a few people knew of the enormous project. When it was completed, the Sioux City base would have a population of more than six thousand people. At that time, the Air Force was still a division of the US Army.

At the Sioux City training base, the stately B-17 Flying Fortresses would soon be joined by stumpy four engine Consolidated B-24 Liberators.

The mission of the Combat Training School in Sioux City was to train entire bombing groups for overseas combat deployment and later for crew replacements. The training objectives included aerial gunnery, formation flying, and, navigation. At the completion of training, the bomber crews and planes hurried to assignments in the hostile skies of Europe, Asia, and the Pacific Islands.

Captain James Stewart, recently from Hollywood, trained in Sioux City before shipping out for Europe where he flew twenty combat missions. Stewart stayed in the US Air Force Reserve after the war and was eventually promoted to Brigadier General. Across Iowa at the Naval Aerial Training Center in Ottumwa, Richard M. Nixon, who would later operate from a much larger runway, was also trained before shipping out to the South Pacific where he earned promotion to Lieutenant Commander.

The gunners sometimes chucked out a few feet of .50 caliber machine gun bullet belts to clear their guns before flying to their targets on the firing range. A .50 caliber shell is about five inches long. It has a lead point surrounding a hardened steel bullet designed to penetrate armor. The brass shell is filled with granular gun powder. The butt end of the shell contains a firing cap. We picked up the live shells off the ground still clipped together into belts ready to feed into the airplane machine guns.

The compulsion for boys to do foolish things with the .50 caliber bullets trumped good judgment. We placed them on top of fence posts and shot at the firing caps with .22 caliber rifle bullets. Once in a while we hit a cap and the bullets fired. We also twisted the bullets out of their brass casements, poured the powder on the ground, and lit it with matches to watch it burn intensely in a crackling, narrow column of fire and smoke. Amazingly, we survived our stupidity.

Consolidated B-24 Liberator

I never tired of running out of the house to watch the planes even though hundreds of formations flew over our farm during the next several years. Near the end of the war, a few of the newer B-29 Super-Fortresses came to Sioux City. The radically improved B-29s could haul two and a half times the payload of B-17s and fly sixty percent farther.

Enough crews were trained in Sioux City and other training centers to man more than 12,000 Flying Fortresses and 18,000 Liberators. Dreadful bomber and crew losses early in the war fell dramatically with improvements in design and tactics and the development and deployment of long range escort fighter planes.

The Sioux City base completed its mission in 1945 and closed. Few people today know of this teeming facility that rose overnight from the Iowa cornfields and then just as quickly fell ghostly silent.

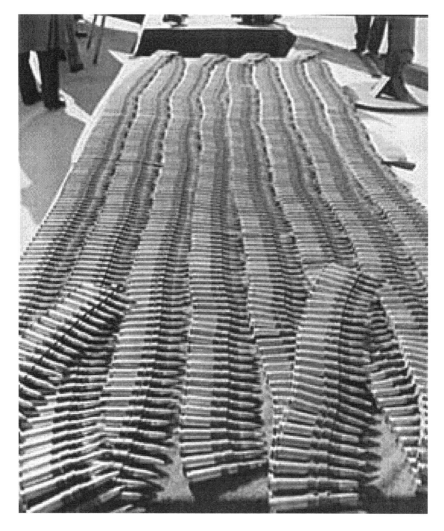

Belts of .50 Caliber Ammunition
Ready to Load into a Flying Fortress

To many, flying in World War II was considered the most glamorous job in the armed services. For us children, secure on our South Dakota farm, the planes and crews were strange and exotic intrusions into our lives. The early flaws in the plane designs and training tactics; airmen stresses and anxieties; and the threats of injury and death were unknown to us. It was much later that we learned of the appalling losses of young crews and often unreliable bombers that briefly passed through the Combat Training School in Sioux City. We assumed the dashing airmen would all return home to glorious and triumphant victory parades in starched uniforms, gleaming brass, and fluttering ribbons as they rode down Main Street in the back seats of convertibles while high-stepping marching bands played "Stars and Stripes Forever."

CHAPTER SEVEN

DOING THE CHORES

Farm chores expand to consume all available labor.

My six brothers, my sister, a hired girl, hired men, and my parents lived on our South Dakota farm in the 1930s. It seemed reasonable that there would be more than enough help available to do all of the daily farm chores—caring for hogs, cattle, horses, and chickens; gardening; building and machinery maintenance; cooking; and household duties. However, farm chores were like the biblical fishes and loaves—they were endless.

Modern electricity and tractors were widely available, but due to the severe economic doldrums and the drought in the Midwest during the Great Depression, they were rare in our community. The use of human power and horse power was largely unchanged for fifty years.

Caring for our five horses was time consuming. Leather harnesses required constant patching and sewing. Horses needed currying to remove hair, mud, and manure. Feeding hay and oats three times a day, seven days a week, was essential. Daily manure removal from stalls had to be attended to. The horses needed medical care—hoof trimming and shoeing; sore shoulder treatment to ease horse collar rubbing; liniment rubs for stiff joints, and axle grease application in summer to protect flesh bitten raw by relentless swarms of hungry flies.

The long-lived horses were usually paired in teams—Mickey and Dobbin and Pat and Pete. Nellie was on standby to fill in for sickness and for occasional use as a saddle horse.

My father had a life-long love affair with horses; woe onto anyone who abused them or neglected to provide for their welfare.

The burden of horse-related chores was offset by the affectionate and gentle companionship of the enormous beasts.

Milk cows required seven days a week of chores. Our five-cow herd amply supplied milk, butter, and cream for household consumption. We sold the excess cream to Keating Creamery where it paid with heavy silver dollars. The skimmed milk remaining at the farm after the cream was separated out was welcomed with noisy, slurpy enthusiasm by the hogs and calves.

We milked the cows by hand into buckets—always from the right side—while we sat on one-legged stools. In fly season, we attached a restraint to the cow's rear legs to prevent foot stomping and kicking. The restraint had a clip for holding the cow's tail to restrict her from switching it. A swish across the face by a course, manure-saturated tail was painful, annoying, and unsanitary.

While milking, a side diversion was squirting a puddle of milk into a pie tin for the anxiously waiting conglomeration of cats. They lived in cozy comfort under the cow manger and earned their keep by killing rodents.

After we milked the cows into three gallon galvanized buckets, we poured it into a round tank on the top of our hand-cranked DeLaval cream separator. The separator parts needed daily washing—another tedious chore.

And there was the boring job of making butter in a wooden-staved churn with a paddle that moved up and down. It seemed to take hours to agitate the milk until butter suddenly appeared. Children, with their minds on more urgent and enjoyable pursuits, could barely endure the monotony. However, a reward was a glass of the refreshing, tangy, buttermilk.

Cows needed feeding, watering, pasturing, and breeding to keep them productive and contented. They also required a lot of cleaning up after; their careless toilet habits were disgraceful.

Our family did not consume all of the available milk. We "served" the excess to the hogs. A hog became a friend for life when it was fed milk. Feeding hogs the kitchen garbage could also develop similar friendships. We were easily motivated to take the kitchen garbage to the hog pens because it was entertaining to dump it over the fence onto the hog's eager, upturned faces with their wide-open mouths. Eating garbage and drinking milk was a highly competitive process for the hogs.

Weaned calves also drank excess milk. We taught them to drink by holding their heads in milk buckets and inserting our fingers into their mouths to simulate cow teats.

Cows occupied a compelling position in the barnyard hierarchy with their graceless but demanding presence. The bossy cow aided in the herd management with her imperious domination of the other cows.

Although the pigs lived in the barnyard with the other animals, they squealed from their own song book. They devoted much of their considerable intelligence to securing food. One of their favorites was slop—barley soaked in fifty-five gallon barrels with water and yeast. After a day in hot weather, the slop quickly fermented making the barrels smell like ripe vats of beer.

As a ten-year-old boy, one of my chores was to carry five-gallon buckets of slop from the barrels to the hog troughs. The first time I did it, the impatient hogs knocked me to the ground and tipped over the bucket.

I could outrun the hogs, so I ran with an empty bucket for bait to an adjoining pen with the pigs in pursuit, switched back, and slammed the gate shut to confine them in the pen until I filled the hog troughs without interference. When I tried this ploy again the second day, the hogs outsmarted me by hedging their bets; half of them followed me into the adjoining pen; the other half stayed and again knocked me down.

When hogs are agitated, they protect themselves by swinging their heads from side to side while slashing with their sharp tusk-like teeth. My brothers and I have numerous hand and leg scars to help us recall our tussles with the hogs as we held them for vaccinations, ear marking, nose-ringing, and conversion of males from boars to barrows.

We took a runt pig aside to nurse it back to health. He lived in our menagerie reserved for pets—pink-eyed, white rabbits, a deodorized

Hogs Dining on Slop

skunk, a squirrel, a rooster, a duck, and a pigeon. He became an affectionate pet and never returned to his litter.

With a show of excessive patriotic zeal, we named the pig Douglas McArthur, in honor of the commanding general of the World War II battles raging in the Pacific Islands and Southeast Asia. It became a challenge to fulfill the pig's desire for cuddling when his poundage passed the two- hundred mark.

In late summer, we harvested wagon loads of unsold watermelons and hauled them to the hog yard. To a hog, melons are fit for the banquet halls of kings. This chore became boyish play when we stood on top of the wagon and exploded the ripe melons like grenades on the ground as close as possible to the hogs' eager upturned snouts.

The chore of gathering, cutting, sawing, splitting, and chopping firewood was like a chronic headache; it never went away. Heating our large drafty house and cooking took an endless supply of firewood.

The chicken house with more than a hundred cackling hens necessitated a staggering amount of chores. The egg-layers filled their laying boxes with eggs a couple times a day. To maintain egg production required the hens to consume large amounts of water, feed, and crushed oyster shells to thicken their shells.

Cleaning up after the hens was the worst of the chicken house chores. Odoriferous, musky chicken droppings make skunk juice smell mild. The distribution of the droppings by the clever chickens defies the laws of statistics. If a chicken deposits one dropping in a hundred acre field, it will invariably fall where a tool will later be dropped. The tool user will not immediately notice the offensive mess smeared on his hands from handling the tool. The god-awful smell will remain embedded on his hands for days even after vigorous scrubbing with Lava soap.

We rubbed the gathered eggs with steel wool to clean them and carefully packed those not consumed at our own table into sturdy wooden egg cases to take to town for cash sale. The cases were made in our Uncle Jack's nearby wood products factory.

Vegetable gardening included all of the burdensome chores well-known since our childhoods when our mother read us *Peter Rabbit* with its stories about the toils of Mr. McGregor. High on our list of miserable garden chores was duck-walking down potato rows to knock beetles off the plant leaves into bean cans partially filled with kerosene. The misery was offset by our childish pleasure of giving the beetles a crackling, smoky cremation when the cans were full.

My father was a tireless and energetic proponent of 4-H clubs (head, hearts, hands, and health.) The clubs taught rural kids many of the lessons that town kids learned through scouting. Boy's 4-H clubs raised animals and crops while keeping careful performance records. Girl's clubs concentrated on sewing and food. 4-H club members were

Buzzsaw Cutting Firewood with
"One Lung" Gasoline Engine

rewarded in late summer when their products were shown and judged at County Achievement Days. The winners could then go on to the State Fair in Huron to compete for higher glory. 4-H club projects generated lots of chores.

Years later when my father died, my brother Pat and his wife Pearl took over our farm. Their first act, while recalling the chores of their youth, was to promptly dispose of the remaining chickens and milk cows and to concentrate their efforts on large-scale, more profitable farming.

CHAPTER EIGHT

THE DAY THEY TURNED ON THE JUICE

When Thomas Edison worked late into the night developing the electric light bulb, he did it by candle light. It made his work seem more urgent.
—George Carlin

Until the mid-twentieth century, when night descended on rural America, everything went black as the inside of a cow's stomach. A few gloomy globes of light provided by candles or kerosene lamps lit supper tables enough to see the food and kerosene lanterns lit cow sheds for evening and early morning milking.

A daily chore was washing the sooty glass lamp chimneys, trimming the wicks, and refilling the glass lamp bases with kerosene. The wicks needed to be carefully adjusted to reduce soot accumulation inside the chimneys.

Lamps and lanterns were dangerous. If tipped over and broken, kerosene ran onto the floor and ignited from the flaming wick. We all know this from the popular legend about Mrs. O'Leary's cow kicking over a kerosene lantern that started the Chicago fire killing hundreds and destroying four square miles of the city.

Power for farm tools and machinery was provided by human muscles or horses turning gears and shafts or by jacked up rear wheels of Model-T Fords or by windmills. On some farms, primitive radios operated with a trickle of power from wind chargers.

After thousands of years of studying the nature of electricity, it came into its own in the 1880s. American farms started to share in the amazing benefits of electricity soon after 1933 when President Franklin D. Roosevelt signed Executive Order 7037 establishing the controversial, but highly successful, Rural Electrification Administration (REA). It provided low interest loans and assistance—mostly through electric cooperatives—to finance power lines and distribution systems for supplying electricity to rural America. The federal government anticipated that the REA would create jobs and stimulate rural economic growth at a time of massive unemployment and prolonged economic doldrums.

My father was a 4-H club promoter, country school board president, and rural fire department founder. After the REA was enacted, he expanded his community service work by encouraging farmers to sign up with the recently established Clay-Union Electric Cooperative.

Although the benefits were obvious to him, this was not so to everyone.

A neighbor would not sign up because the power line right-of-way would disturb his grove of gnarled, short-lived mulberry trees. Two other neighbors, who had a history of discord with each other, couldn't agree on the location of a shared transformer. My father was a persuasive man; he soon solicited their signatures and enough others so the local cooperative could proceed with design and construction of a neighborhood REA power grid. The power to feed the grid was bought from existing power generating companies.

Existing, privately-owned power companies that served urban customers seldom distributed power to rural areas on the grounds that revenues and profits were insufficient. The power companies often resisted the REA out of fear of encroachment onto their turf.

However, if the power companies thought hooking up a farmer was a lead-pipe cinch for them to earn a profit, they gave in. My grandfather operated a large farm and a dairy near the South Dakota State Mental Health Asylum. Northwestern Public Service power lines serving the asylum ran directly by his farmstead. In 1913 when he contracted to invest $1,000 in electrically operated equipment on his farm, the power company relented and allowed him to become their customer.

Reddy Kilowatt
REA Logo

The excitement in rural homes was palpable as power line poles were set and wires pulled. The idea of having bright lights, washing machines, radios, irons, vacuum cleaners, and refrigerators was beyond the dreams of most farm and ranch families.

In anticipation of the arrival of electricity, houses and barns were wired at a fast pace to be ready for the wondrous electricity. It was not uncommon to run pairs of wires with braided insulation across house ceilings to white porcelain fixtures with bare sixty-watt bulbs. The wires were supported on split white porcelain insulators held in place with eight-penny nails driven through plaster into wall studs and ceiling joists. The novelty and pleasure of having electricity just like the town folk trumped aesthetic considerations.

House Wiring for the REA

When prosperity started to return to rural America, electricity soon powered washing machines, cream separators, shop drills and tools, pumps, milking machines, and furnace fans.

A few prosperous and adventurous farmers even installed water pumping systems for operating "indoor plumbing." However, some older men never became accustomed to indoor plumbing; they still "did their duty" outside as they always had.

The day they "turned on the juice" was as well remembered to rural people as Armistice Day, New Years Day, or Independence Day. The biblical expression, "And let there be light," now had tangible meaning. It meant liberation from darkness, scrub boards, cisterns for cooling food, smelly chamber pots, and hand-cranked tools and implements.

A few farmers, such as my parents, had primitive 32 volt, DC Delco generators run with a single-cylinder gasoline engine that stored energy in square glass jars containing acid and lead cells. Even for them, modern

110 volt AC power was an enormous leap forward. They were no longer restricted to a few dim, low wattage lights and a static-prone radio. My brother, Pat, recalls, "When the batteries were low on the 32 volt system, you had to light a match to see if the bulbs were on."

After the miracle of electric power finally was firmly established in rural America, outhouses were abandoned to rot or become garden tool sheds; kerosene lamps were stored and later sold as antiques; chamber pots became flower pots; windmill blades spun until they wore out and fell to the ground and the towers became trellises for wild vines; and the crystal set and early vacuum tube radios became curiosities stored away on top closet shelves.

Because the REA made electricity available on farms and ranches throughout America, the quality of domestic life dramatically improved. More efficient farm and ranch methods were put in place just in time to support the enormous forthcoming demand for agricultural products during World War II. Hired girls traditionally employed for household work left to work in factories. Hired farm hands were drafted into military service. Farmers and ranchers were better able to cope since electricity was now available to ease their work.

By 1945 half of American farms had electricity; by 1980, 80 percent were hooked up.

To this day, seventy years later, most farmers and ranchers still sing praise for the federal government's foresight in enacting the REA. It went a long way to reduce the disparity between rural and city living.

CHAPTER NINE

THE DAY THE NEW TRACTOR CAME

I am not convinced that the tractor will ever replace the horse.
—William Butterworth, President of Deere and Co.
(From 1918 Board of Directors Meeting minutes when John Deere deliberated purchasing Waterloo Gasoline Engine Co., a tractor manufacturing firm.)

A friend, who is a marketing manager for John Deere, recently returned from a business trip to India where the company manufactures agricultural tractors developed for local Indian market conditions. My friend accompanied a dealer as he delivered a new tractor to a farm. The farmstead was festooned with garlands. The occasion was attended by family and friends. Tables of celebratory food and refreshments were set out. A holy man was present to bless the occasion and pray for good fortune and prosperity.

The reception in India for a new tractor seemed like a quaint ceremony. But I then recalled our South Dakota farm. August 2, 1942, was a day of jubilation. A truck from Binns Implement Company, an International Harvester farm equipment dealer, turned down our dirt road to deliver a spotless, bright red, Model-H Farmall (International Harvester Company) tractor. We had no unloading dock so the driver backed his truck into the road ditch and made a height adjustment in the sandy soil with a shovel so he could back the awesome new machine off the truck and drive it down the cedar tree lined driveway to our farmyard.

My father wrote a check to Clarence Binns for $667.50 for the new tractor. The original cancelled check is still in an upstairs storeroom of

Model-H Farmall Tractor

our century-old farmhouse along with all the other checks written since the late 1920s.

My brothers and I watched the arrival of this marvelous new machine with no less excitement than the Indian farmer when his new tractor was delivered.

When the Chariot of the Gods arrived long ago from outer space, it could not have seemed grander than our new tractor.

Massive industrial mobilization for World War II was just getting underway. The government materiel control authorities embargoed everything critical for supplying the military services of the U.S. and its allies. This included rubber and batteries. The new tractor ran on clunky steel wheels with lethal-looking lugs and depended on a hand crank for starting. The transmission gear for running the tractor at high speed—fifteen miles per hour—was omitted.

To fill the voracious wartime appetite for iron to feed the foundries of America, we junked our clumsy pre-World War I Waterloo Boy (later to become John Deere) tractor during one of the frequent patriotic scrap metal drives.

My father let my brothers and me take the tractor for a short spin around the farmyard. The excitement was palpable. The smell of fresh paint, still in the final curing stage from the engine heat, lingers in my memory after all of these years. The burbling exhaust system sound was like a lullaby when the engine idled. That our father had enough confidence to entrust us with his prized new tractor was exhilarating.

We'd no longer need to do the horse chores. The tractor would only need fueling, oil changing, and greasing. During idle times, the tractor would be content to stand unattended.

Our father was less excited than we were. He knew that to keep up with the times and remain economically competitive, he had to switch from horsepower to tractor power, but he hated to see his beloved horses put out to pasture—or worse, to be hauled off to the rendering works.

It would not do to leave our fine new tractor out in the weather when not in use. We modified a stall in the machine shed for storing it.

For the next weeks, we stared at the new tractor in awe and could think and talk of little else. We examined every detail and learned how the controls worked. It was fun to turn the steering wheel fully to one side, jam on one of the individual rear wheel brakes, and spin the tractor around in a tight circle while pivoting on one rear wheel.

Seventy years later the Model-H Farmall tractor is still on the farm—well maintained and painted—performing light tasks and providing rides around the farmyard for countless grandchildren, nieces, nephews, and visitors.

Although Farmall was the brand name used by the International Harvester Company for its tractors, they were so predominant that some farmers used Farmall as the generic name for all tractor brands.

Waterloo Boy Tractor
Ready for a Parade

At first our new tractor towed wagons and farm equipment and turned its pulley to run a feed grinder, buzz saw, and silage chopper. Soon other equipment was mounted on the tractor such as a cultivator and end loader. Equipment that was previously driven by ground-engaging wheels—manure spreader, corn binder, and grain binder—was now driven with the tractor power takeoff shaft.

No acquisition later in life would ever be as exciting to us young farm boys as the day the shiny new Farmall tractor came to our farm.

As soon as World War II ended, our Farmall was updated with rubber tires, a battery, an electric starter, and a gear for high speed travel.

Tractors and other related powered equipment—accompanied by seed hybridization and irrigation—started a food production revolution that still goes on today with no end in sight. The world of agriculture is changing at a faster rate today than at any time since nine thousand BC when man first domesticated plants.

CHAPTER TEN

THE DAY THE COW DANCED ON ME

Down by the sliprails (gate) stands our cow
Chewing, chewing, chewing,
She does not care what folks out there
In the great, big world are doing.

—C.J. Dennis

The buildings on our South Dakota farm were dominated by an eighty-foot long red barn with white trim and topped by a pair of ventilator cupolas and a trotting horse weather vane.

Through the middle of the barn ran an alley with access by a pair of sliding doors large enough for a horse drawn hayrack piled with hay to unload into the second floor haymow.

The barn alley also served as a temporary refuge for cows with new-born calves. On a cold, blustery day in 1937, our Holstein cow—part of our five cow milking herd—temporarily resided in the alley where she anxiously tended her new-born calf. The cow's name was "Holstein." She was known for her docile behavior.

My brothers and I liked to look at and play with newborn farm animals—calves, foals, piglets kittens, chicks, ducklings, bunnies, and puppies. Gene and I returned home in late afternoon from school; the country schoolhouse was less than a minute's run from our farmhouse. We wolfed down a slab of homemade bread topped with butter and jam.

Gene said, "Let's go look at Holstein's new calf."

I said, "OK, but we can't let Roly come into the barn. Holstein will think her calf is being attacked by a wolf." We rolled the doors shut after

Holstein

we entered the barn alley to pet the calf, but there was a board loose on the door. Roly stuck his nose in through the opening.

Holstein's primordial instincts shifted into high gear; she ran at Roly to defend her calf. She could not get to him so she attacked me. She butted me to the floor and "danced" over me. When I looked up at her belly; it blotted out the view of the entire barn ceiling. Each hoof pressed down with three hundred pounds of pressure. She fractured my skull and cut open my left cheek.

Gene frantically ran outside and screamed for help. My father was just leaving the barnyard on his way to a field with a load of manure

Roly

pulled by a team of big, gentle Percheron horses. He heard Gene's shrill screams over the howling wind. He ran into the barn. Holstein, still agitated, also knocked him down but did not hurt him.

The pigeons roosting in the steel hay rail in the roof peak did not give a fig about the drama going on below as they continued to coo and jostle each other.

My father and Gene led me into the house and sat me on a kitchen chair. My vision was blurred because of swelling and bleeding. My father put a white dishcloth into the wood-fired kitchen stove oven to disinfect it before he wrapped my head. My mother was in town for her weekly grocery shopping.

He rang the telephone operator and told her to connect him to 27F5, the number for my Uncle Francis. "Come right away, Francis is hurt and Mary is in town with our car. We need to get him to a doctor in a hurry. He's hurt pretty bad."

While we waited, I built up a puff of air pressure in my mouth and was surprised that my tattered cheek "blubbered" and spattered blood on the linoleum floor.

Uncle Francis arrived in his Buick and started to drive me, along with my father, to Sacred Heart Hospital four miles away in Yankton. I knew my father was concerned about me because he did not smoke his usual pipe or cigar in the car. The smoke always made me sick. Even though I was dripping blood as it seeped through the towel around my head, I tried to sit up to see out the windshield. I had no pain and little concern for my condition; it seemed like an adventure.

My mother was driving home with the week's groceries. She saw us when my father waved at her to stop. He ran to her car and roughly pulled her out by the arm. "Francis is hurt bad; get in the other car with him!"

She saw the bandage around my head and asked, "Is it his eye?" It wasn't.

The doctor sewed my cheek up with as much finesse as if he was stitching up the back end of a holiday goose. My cheek would remain hard and lumpy for months. The stitch marks made my face look like it was laced together with boot strings.

After we reached the hospital and Doctor Treweiler treated me, my mother asked, "Will he be okay?"

He cautiously answered, "Mary, we will do all we can." He was concerned about my skull fracture. Eventually nature pushed the crushed skull bone back out to its normal position.

He had other recent experience with cattle injuries. He treated Dr. Smith, my Aunt Helen's father, who was tragically trampled by his own bull. Dr. Treweiler could not save him.

Later in the evening when my father returned to look after his horses, they had not moved a step as they customarily would have.

I stayed in the hospital for eight days, my mother stayed with me the first several nights. The art of cleaning wounds was less stringent than today. A few days later, I fingered my cheek wound and dislodged a barnyard straw. My head looked as big as a prize cabbage at the State Fair. My eyes were swollen shut, and I could only open my mouth enough for a straw.

While I was in the hospital, I received a small book entitled *The Blue Book of Dogs* with a pair of black and white Scotties on its blue cover. On the fly leaf was written: Hope you'll soon be back at school with us, Francis. It was signed: From the Willowdale pupils. I cherished the book; seventy four years later it is still on my bookshelf.

After celebrating my eighth birthday in the hospital, I was discharged and returned to school with a four inch square bandage taped to my cheek. I was briefly the object of curiosity among my eighteen schoolmates.

My doctor advised me to massage my cheek scar to make it subside. This treatment was of no apparent benefit, and my attention span did not allow me to continue rubbing for more than a week. In later years, when I started earning income in my professional life, I considered having the scar surgically removed, but by then, it had been with me for so long, I decided to let it go.

One of the more tedious farm chores was milking cows. My father thought I was afraid of cows after my accident; he never again asked me to milk the cows. I did not tell him I had no fear whatsoever of cows. Some of my brothers thought I was a slacker; perhaps I was.

While I was in my mid-thirties, my company asked me to move with my family to Mannheim, Germany to manage the building of an iron foundry. Most Germans who looked at my face assumed I was a German University student who received my scar while dueling to defend a point of honor. At that time, the Germans still regarded dueling scars as "a mark of gentlemanly bravery." Some rubbed salt in to their fresh "trophies of honor" to make them heal poorly and look fiercer. Before moving to Germany, I hired a tutor to teach me to speak German. With Teutonic forthrightness, and apparently in expectation of an exotic explanation, Frau Schuler asked, "How did you come by that facial scar?" When I explained that it happened the day our Holstein cow danced on me, she incredulously said, *"Eine Kuh-unglaublich!"* ("A cow! Unbelievable!")

CHAPTER ELEVEN

DOMESTIC LIFE ON THE FARM

Down on a old gravel road
On a hill I go home
To visit the reasons
I don't feel alone.

—Connetta Jean

Even though the economy of the country collapsed during the Great Depression of the 1930s, my parents learned how to function virtually on a non-cash basis. They canceled their checking account and kept their meager cache of bills and coins in an empty Prince Albert tobacco tin on top of the kitchen cabinet. They purchased only staple groceries such as salt, flour, and sugar.

Nevertheless, we had a bountiful table supplied with our own farm-grown vegetables—lettuce, carrots, beets, radishes, beans, peas, tomatoes, potatoes, squash, melons, strawberries, rhubarb, and corn. And fruit came from our orchards—apples, cherries, plums, mulberries, elder-berries, and pears.

From our livestock yards we had an ample supply of chicken, pork, and beef. Fresh milk, cream, and butter were always on hand from our herd of five milk cows.

We liked to gulp milk down while it was still warm and foamy from the cow-in fact we often squirted it directly from the cow's teats into our open mouths. We also served milk to the eager, open-mouthed cats the same way.

We stored potatoes and squash in bins in the cellar. Carrots lasted a long time after harvest when packed in sand-filled barrels. It was nip and tuck if the potatoes would survive in the basement bins until the first new potatoes were available the next season. The reeking smell of rotting potatoes that did not last the season was memorable. Removing the spoiled potatoes from their storage bins was not a reward offered for good behavior.

My mother and Leona Kast, our hired girl, baked bread once a week in our wood-fired Monarch range; this cream-colored monument dominated our kitchen. Even though each housewife used similar bread recipes, the children could always tell the difference between the bakers; Grandma's bread tasted "different."

Although hunger was rampant for many city people who could not find employment, few farm families ever went to bed hungry.

Pocket watches were rare, so alternatives were used for determining time. Each town set off its siren at noon. The siren at the nearby village of Mission Hill was the most audible on our farm. Noon could also be determined by making a human sundial; standing with arms outstretched in a north–south orientation. When a shadow was cast directly down, it was noon. Sturdy cast-iron bells announced meals and emergencies on some farms.

Our family and hired help ate meals together three times a day. In cold weather we ate in the kitchen at a heavy, oak table and in summer on the north porch. On Sundays and holidays and when company came, we ate in our dining room with everyone dressed in their best clothes.

After Sunday dinner, afternoons were free for pursuing personal interests; swimming in a neighbor's artesian water pool, playing black jack, fishing, hunting, or shooting air rifles and slingshots.

Blackjack bets usually were made with .22 caliber rifle bullets. Rifles were seldom misused—if pot shots at roadside signs and barn weather vanes are excluded from consideration.

Fishing from the muddy banks of the languid Jim River was good Sunday entertainment. We fished with scraps of string wrapped around corncobs, nuts and washers for weights, freshly dug earth worms for bait, and store-bought hooks. Sunfish, bass, catfish, carp, and bullheads were the prey. On warm days, fishing was soon superseded by cannon ball jumps into the water as a prelude to swimming, rafting on floating logs, and horseplay.

In the summer, our yard became an extension of the house living space. A metal wash stand stood on the lawn—if mowed weeds could be called a lawn—for pre-meal washing up. A long bench stood on the wide concrete step on the shady side of the house. Farm hands sat on a bench after meals to rest, smoke, and quietly discuss the work of the day. The yard was shaded by towering cottonwood trees.

Meal times were the occasion for conversations. My father sat at one end of the table and spoke of farm affairs, livestock prices, and weather. My mother used her seat at the other end of the table as her podium for teaching manners and English usage; commenting on the beauty of nature; and discussing education. She never let us forget that she had once been a school teacher.

After dinner, the children stretched out on the living room floor for short naps. My parents rested briefly on a sofa or bed. Napping abruptly ended when my father shouted, "Time to get up!" or "Let's hitch up!"

We sometimes had our haircuts administered in the house yard by Red Costello, a farmhand who had a hair clipper and "homemade" hair cutting skill. The lopsided results sometimes made us look like we were born with head deformities.

Near the front of the house stood the "old house" that served as a summer kitchen and laundry room. It was set up with a four-burner kerosene cook stove, a Maytag washing machine, a DeLaval cream separator, and various paraphernalia for canning vegetables, fruits, and meat. Innumerable chickens were beheaded, scalded to remove their feathers, and cooked in the "old house." A chopping block and axe stood outside the door. The boys showed their weird nature by counting the number of times a chicken could aimlessly hop after decapitation. The main house was much more endurable during hot weather because of the summer kitchen.

An open-sided wood shed was connected to the "old house." The shed stored chopped wood and corncobs. The household consumed huge quantities of cobs and wood for heating and cooking.

Delaval Cream Separator

On Saturdays, my mother and Leona baked cinnamon rolls for Sunday breakfast. They made the rolls with heavy-handed portions of brown sugar, butter, and nuts. What a treat!

On Saturday afternoons my mother or Leona scrubbed and waxed the linoleum kitchen floor and "protected it from harm" until Sunday morning with newspapers. Just before bedtime my mother cleaned the kitchen range and rubbed it with wads of waxed paper to make its black cooking surfaces shine. Sunday morning, before the family arose, she removed the newspapers. The floor and stove stood for a brief moment in sparkling glory. The children also "shone"; they would not yet have accumulated a new coat of dirt since their baths the previous evening. The family, after completing the morning farm chores, dressed in their best clothes for church and sat down to an abundant breakfast with the centerpiece of warm cinnamon rolls. Sunday dinners usually included invited relatives. They were minor celebrations.

After attending Christmas Midnight Mass on cold, crisp, winter nights, the family returned home to an oyster stew meal. Usually a few neighbors stopped by to share the stew. It was surprising that a market existed for fresh oysters so far from their seashore origin; there was such a demand that a system was in place to deliver barrels of oysters by fast freight to the Midwest.

Modern refrigerators were not yet available. An icebox cooled our food in summer. We bought fifty-pound cakes of ice in town weekly at the Pure Ice Company and hauled them home wedged between the car fender and front bumper. It was always the last item bought to reduce melting on the way home.

At the Lyons grandparents' house, they placed butter and milk in a bucket and lowered it by rope into the cistern to cool. They had no source for ice.

"Two-hole outhouses" were the rural standard for toilets. Outhouses were located a distance from the farmhouse that slightly exceeded their pungency limit. One hole was smaller than the other for the convenience of children. In the winter, chamber pots were set on newspapers in each bedroom. The men of the family mostly attended to their toilet needs alfresco in the woods or behind the barn. Outhouses were the source of countless rural pranks and jokes. Fastidious people poured lime down the holes of the outhouses to control the aroma.

Housewives sometimes planted hollyhocks along the path near the door. Obsolete catalogues, newspapers, and corncobs were the source for toilet paper. Store-bought toilet paper was a rare luxury.

The family took Saturday night baths in a white, cast iron bathtub with water heated on the kitchen range. Most of the children bathed in the same water. As many boys as would fit were put in the tub; it was a form of water sport.

On special occasions such as birthdays and holidays, we made ice cream in a hand-cranked freezer; it was a long and boring process. The freezer was a wooden-staved bucket with a crank and mechanism for rotating a cylindrical tank filled with raw ingredients—eggs, cream, and flavoring. The tank turned in ice and salt until its contents froze into ice cream that tasted like the nectar of the gods.

Honey, still in the wax combs, was a staple on our table during the winter. Bill Volmer, our family barber, was a beekeeper. He kept his hives on our farm and gave us a five-gallon milk can of honey each fall.

The older boys sometimes wore clothes that came from a bale of World War I surplus military uniforms. Scarcely-known relatives sent the bales from Norwich, Vermont. The wool khakis shirts were too big so we turned up the cuffs. The clothes cache included heavy army overcoats. As we grew older and the overcoats started to fit, we wore them on the farm during winter weather. The overcoats made us look like Napoleon's retreating army after his winter defeat in Moscow.

On trips to distant hay fields in bitter winter weather, we drove the horses from high atop loaded hayracks with the army overcoats piled around us. It was always colder on the way home due to the sweat generated while pitching the hay onto the hayracks. No amount of overcoats was ever enough for warmth.

The normal "uniform" for the Willowdale School boys was striped, bib overalls. In the fall my mother bought new overalls for us from J.C. Penney or Montgomery Ward stores. We wore our new overalls during the school year and then for farm work the following summer.

Bib overalls could be "jazzed up" with beer and pop bottle caps. The caps were held in place by reinserting the cork seals inside the bib behind the caps. Bob Walsh held the record with forty caps emblazoned on his bib overalls and ten on his felt cap. He strutted around school in his self-made finery as if he was a monarch dressed in ermine.

One fall my mother acquired light colored trousers for us to wear to school. We vetoed wearing the trousers because we would look different from the other children. Finally, my mother negotiated a deal; she promised that if we wore the trousers on the first morning of the fall term and still disliked them, we could revert to bib overalls when we came home at noon for dinner. We rushed home, tore off our trousers, and put on our overalls so it would no longer be necessary to face the other school children in different looking clothes. Our mother never reneged on a deal.

An item of universal winter wear was the subject of many jokes; "long-handled underwear"—also called "Long Johns." A suit of underwear was an ankle to neck, thick cotton garment with rubber buttons up the front and a button-up rear "trap door." Some said there were people who sewed their children into their long underwear in the fall and cut them out in the spring. With the inadequate heating systems of the day and the need for extensive time outside, the underwear was a necessity.

Boys typically wore high work shoes that came up over their ankles. The long shoelaces were threaded through eyelets on the bottom half of the shoe and looped over hooks on the top half. The hooks enabled great speed in putting on and taking off the shoes without the need for untying laces.

My eldest brother Pat was usually the only one to wear new clothes; the rest of us wore his hand-me-downs. The useful remains of worn out garments made patch material.

Stockings were always a problem with worn out heels and toes in the days before long-wearing fabrics. Mending socks was a task for evenings or spare moments. Occasionally Grandma took a basket full of stockings home for mending.

The Federal Rural Electrification Authority (REA) introduced electricity throughout rural America in the early 1940s. It was a day of indescribable pleasure when "they first turned on the juice." Rural America could now have adequate lights, refrigerators, and radios.

Monday was laundry day. Laundering was a lengthy and messy process-especially in the wintertime. My mother washed clothes in a Maytag washing machine driven by a smelly, noisy gasoline engine or a 32 volt electric motor. In winter, light-weight clothes dried in the heated rooms of the house. The house smelled pungent and moist on laundry days. She hung heavier clothes on the outside clotheslines for several days to dry in the icy winter wind.

In good weather, all of the clothes were dried on clotheslines in the back yard. My mother had a good-natured running battle with the wrens that used her canvas clothespin bags as a nesting place. Once in a while an escaped cow wondered under the low hanging clothes lines knocking the clothes to the ground. To paraphrase Mark Twain, "Words were then spoken that even a blue jay wouldn't say."

People normally changed their clothes once each week after their Saturday evening bath. More frequent changing was impractical due to the labor-intensive washing process.

My mother made laundry soap from a mixture of beef tallow and lye. It worked okay, but it would have challenged soap advertising writers to favorably describe its appearance and smell.

Irons were heated on the kitchen range. Many a shirt had burn marks from overheated irons used by beginners.

When the local newspaper arrived in our roadside mailbox it was an important daily event because it provided the latest installment of the comic strips such as Dick Tracy, Little Orphan Annie, and Red Ryder. We laid the papers out on the floor to read them on our hands and knees with our rumps in the air like ducklings bobbing on a pond for food.

Little-Big Books contained popular boys' adventure stories. The books were small but thick. They had a bonus feature; on the upper right corner of each page was a cartoon figure. The illusion of motion occurred when the pages were rapidly flicked.

Hoping for Some Good News
—Franklin D. Roosevelt Museum

Radio programs geared for children—Jack Armstrong, The All American Boy; Captain Midnight, and Terry and the Pirates—were broadcast late in the afternoon after school. Companies that sponsored the broadcasts extolled the benefits of their brand of breakfast cereals and implied that the implausible exploits of the story heroes were possible because they ate the advertised products. My parents recognized our intense interest in these episodes and allowed us to listen to them while eating a snack of bread and jam before we went outside to do our evening farm chores.

Farming was normally the domain of men. Nevertheless there were cases where women operated farms without a husband or dominant male. Usually this only happened when the woman had a strong farm background. Aunt Ruth, who was city born, had trouble getting her male farm hands to follow her directions after my Uncle Francis died. This forced her to rent out her farm and move to town.

It was customary for most farmers to go to town on Saturday nights to shop. It also gave them the opportunity to chat with neighbors and friends. After shopping, people sat in their cars parked diagonally at the curbs in front of the stores on Main Street. As their friends walked by, they stopped to chat. Some of the more avid talkers and accomplished gossipers came to town early so they could secure the best parking places.

Our large house and the extensive farm buildings offered many places for us to play and exercise our youthful imaginations. An easily climbable catalpa tree stood near our house. The long, slim banana-like seedpods made good spears for hurling at each other. Immense cottonwood trees shaded the entire farmyard and gave relief from the heat during the almost unbearably hot summer months.

We built a tree house in a sprawling willow tree with its branches hanging over the artesian well pond. It was our private refuge. For the younger children, it was a scary inner sanctum in the world of the "big kids." They were occasionally allowed to enter our exciting kingdom.

In addition to the amusement opportunities for children on the farm there were also opportunities for mischief. When horses have their rumps stroked, they relax and arch their tails. We were amused—but not the horses—when we placed sticks under their tails. The horses vigorously clamped their tails down on the sticks and jumped around in a high state of agitation until their tail muscles became exhausted and the sticks fell away.

Rotten chicken eggs, found in abandoned nesting places, have a foul, overwhelming, sulfurous smell when they are broken. It was great fun to lob the rotten eggs at any available target such as a passing animal—or even a brother who was momentarily out of favor.

Another opportunity for mischief was to identify an unsuspecting chicken and feed it a worm with a string tied around its waist (Do worms have waist?). After the chicken swallowed the worm, we pulled it back up. The chickens were slow learners and quite tolerant of this mischief because they allowed encores with the same worm.

Smoking at an early age was something that was considered adventuresome and a rite of passage to adolescence. One day after school, my brother Gene and I tried smoking cigarettes supplied by an older student. The cigarettes were made from Bull Durham tobacco. After two cigarettes, I became sick and threw up; I never did get over tobacco intolerance. Bull Durham was the accepted "he-man's" tobacco. "Cool" farmhands carried a small sack of Bull Durham tobacco in their shirt pocket with its draw string and distinctive round tag hanging out like the price tag on Minnie Pearl's hats.

A hand-operated windshield wiper on my parents' 1928 Dodge car removed exterior moisture. But in winter, frost formed inside the windshield. My father melted it by rubbing on the glass with a small cloth bag filled with salt. The salt melted the ice but caused heavy rusting of the dashboard.

Starting cars in cold weather was doubtful. We pre-heated the carburetor with a blowtorch to vaporize the gasoline and expedite starting. If that did not work a team of horses towed the car to start it.

Operating a car in winter was not made any easier because alcohol was used as radiator coolant. It boiled at a temperature much lower than water making it difficult to prevent radiator overflow.

Cars usually did not have heaters; traveling in winter was only slightly more comfortable than in a wagon or sled. Blankets helped marginally.

In the mid-1940s locker plant services became prevalent for storing fresh meat. The locker plants consisted of walk-in refrigerated rooms with locked drawers and shelves for customers' individual meat storage.

"The Big Kids"—Pat, Francis, and Gene and
"The Little Kids"—Tommie, Betty, Bobbie,
and Jackie Lyons—1943

The locker plant owners were usually butchers; farmers brought their livestock to them for slaughtering and packaging and freezing the meat according to their preferences. Later, as home freezers became common, the locker plants phased out.

Our dinner table always had ten to fifteen "eaters" around it three times a day—a "litter" of seven children, parents, hired girls, farm hands, relatives, and visitors.

There was a nine year age difference from my youngest to my oldest sibling. My mother said, "The stork stopped coming to our house in the late 1930s when Bobbie and Betty (twins) were born."

The hubbub with so many people in our home seemed normal. At a later time when I lived in a college dormitory and military barracks, it also seemed normal. Living alone did not.

Pat, Gene, and I were called "the big kids." Jackie, Tommie, Bobbie, and Betty were called "the little kids." There were a couple years without a stork visit between the two groups.

When conflicts occurred, our home was a safe haven of calm where difficulties were resolved by my parents with an even and balanced hand. To say, "But he started it," was not a valid defense for conflicts.

With the never-ending need for chores to be done on our farm, only a very foolish child ever whined, "I don't have anything to do."

Our home was a happy place with constant companionship, nurturing, encouragement, humor, teaching, learning, laughing, clamoring, bickering, confidence building, value setting, and freedom.

CHAPTER TWELVE

THINGS TO MAKE LIFE BETTER ON THE FARM

Farming looks mighty easy when your plow is a pencil
and you're a thousand miles from the corn field.
—Dwight D. Eisenhower

In the 1930s and 1940s, it had been seventy years since the vast Dakota Territory was first organized. Although farms were well established in most rural areas by this time, they still lacked many of the things common in urban communities.

FARM LOANS

My first memory as a child was of riding on the seat of a one-row, cultivator towed by my father behind a horse drawn wagon. A man asked me, "How old are you?"

"I'm four, and I'm goin' to ride all the way home on our new cul'vator," I answered. Our farm was a half mile away down a narrow dirt road.

My father bought the cultivator for a dollar and a half after making a "pity bid" at the Schoener farm auction. The Schoeners went bust on their arid, sandy farm that could only produce a miserable crop of cockleburs and sunflowers. All else withered and died in the sandy soil blown into dunes during the searing drought of the 1930s. They gave up farming and auctioned off their meager possessions for a few dollars.

The bank that held the Schoener farm mortgage reluctantly added it to its long inventory of unwanted property.

The Grim Day the Bank
Foreclosed on His Farm Loan

President Roosevelt introduced farm credit legislation that was successful—after a dispute with the Supreme Court—in reducing the glut of farm bankruptcies, but it was too late to help the unfortunate Shoeners.

Farm credit was the only way for many to ever own their farms, but when times turned sour, the taste was bitter.

ELECTRIC POWER

Electrical power was almost never available in rural areas. Kerosene lamps or candles lit most farmhouses. If outside work needed to be done in the dark, kerosene lanterns cast enough feeble light to see a path. A few farmers owned devices for generating electricity from wind generators that supplied power to operate radios; and in rare instances, home generators that produced enough electricity to light dim 32 volt bulbs.

At a later time, my father was a stem-winder for urging neighbors to sign up for modern electric service after the passing of the Rural Electrification Authority (REA). Officials would not build rural power lines until enough people agreed to buy electricity. After a day of canvassing for signatures my father said at the supper table, "Well, we now have enough signatures. We're going to be hooked up soon."

HEATING FUEL

Natural gas service was never available for farms. Farmers fueled their furnaces and stoves with wood or occasionally with coal when times were good. Kitchen ranges burned corn cobs and wood; corn cobs were good kindling and gave instant heat.

Outside, kerosene-fueled burners heated animal water tanks to prevent freezing and hoods to warm newly hatched chicks in early spring. Woe unto the boy who shirked on his chores and forgot to fill the animal water tank burners on cold nights; the animals went thirsty and expensive galvanized sheet metal tanks burst.

If a cold spell came during hog farrowing time, we lit a fire in a small cast iron stove in the hog house; with luck the temperature rise was perceptible.

The Northern Natural Gas Company built a pipeline through our farm from the gas producing fields in the south. The strange trench digging and pipe laying equipment and the southern accents of the workers entertained us for the summer during construction.

We were shocked to hear about one of the southern construction workers throwing a heavy, china coffee cup at a respected African-American neighbor in Balfany's Diner explaining, "I don't never eat in no place where they let n——-s come through the door."

Many years later, our farm connected to the natural gas line, a hundred yards distant, to heat the house and farm buildings.

FIRE PROTECTION

The lack of fire protection in our rural neighborhood worried my father. Before he went to bed after burning old corn stalks, he always put on his hat and walked to his fields. "I'm going out to check that a fire hasn't flared up," he said.

If a building or field caught fire, extinction was limited to the efforts of the farmers and neighbors; but there was not much they could do once fires started. On pasture lands where grass fires were common, plowed strips of land helped to stop the spread of fires. But the firebreaks were of little use in high winds; live embers could easily jump over them.

Rural fires were excruciatingly difficult for farmers. They seldom bought insurance or set aside financial reserves.

One evening when my parents talked things over after supper, my father said, "Mary, I read in *The Furrow* magazine about a group of farmers who organized a rural fire association. I wonder if we could get one going here. If a fire starts, we have no protection. We could end up like your brother Will when his farmhouse burned down. "

My mother said, "Well, you are able to get things done on the school board and you were a big part of organizing the neighborhood for electricity, so why not give it a try? The biggest problem will be getting people to shell out the money for membership. Some of them are tighter than the bark on a tree, and some simply don't have the money."

With my father's leadership, Yankton County farmers organized a Rural Fire Association. The largest cost was for a new fire truck.

A fire truck salesman got wind of a pending new truck purchase. He persisted in calling on my father and offering him a free steak dinner. "If I take him up on the free dinner, then I'll owe him something in return. I think I'll buy my own steak dinners," my father said at the supper table.

When the fire association went into operation, it maintained an active schedule putting out fires when tractors, combines, farm buildings, and fields burned. A dilemma arose that never was fully resolved: what to do about fires on property where the owners were not willing to pay the Fire Association membership fee.

ROADS

In the summer, big Caterpillar patrols (road graders) occasionally roared down our newly-built dirt road to fill in the ruts left by cars, trucks, and wagons. The scraper blades also sheared off the weeds growing between the vehicle wheel tracks. In winter an occasional snow plow came by. Gravel roads were a luxury; hard-surface roads were a town thing.

EDUCATION

Education for eight grades was offered in a one-room school house located on the corner of our farm. One teacher taught all eight grades.

My parents strongly encouraged continued education after the eighth grade. Their seven children all continued with their high school education and then went on to numerous colleges and universities.

POLICE PROTECTION

An elected sheriff provided county police protection. Sheriff's duties were mostly for handling thefts, unruly drunks, and road accidents. Road safety was not helped any because the state did not require or offer drivers' licenses. Rural children drove cars as soon as they were big enough to reach the pedals.

The sheriff's job was more to restore calm than punish or fine law breakers.

Bill Hickey was the sheriff of Yankton County for many years. My brother Pat remembers, as a little boy, sitting behind Sheriff Hickey's desk in the county court house. After a few rotations in his oak swivel chair, he read the open arrest log and said, "Look here! It says that George Washington was arrested Saturday night because he got drunk."

TELEPHONES

Although telephones were widely in use for a half century, fewer than ten percent of the people of rural Yankton County were hooked up for service. Telephone working parts were enclosed in a breadbox sized oak case that hung on the wall of dining rooms or living rooms in a place where the user could stand while talking.

Telephone operators placed calls by plugging in wires to complete the circuit to the person called. Rural party lines were shared by about ten people. Each subscriber was assigned a unique combination of short and long rings. Our telephone calls were identified by two "longs." Our number was 18F20; the "F" designated a farm subscriber.

For some on the party line, the temptation to eavesdrop was irresistible. Those who habitually listened to other people's conversations were well known and the object of community ridicule.

Some tried to shame the eavesdroppers into hanging up by having someone shout in the background, "Is Elsie—or whoever—rubber neck-ing on the line again?"

Hello! Operator?

In isolated areas, the top wire of roadside "bob wire" fences transmitted telephone signals. The elimination of telephone line investment was offset by drastically reduced reliability. An open gate broke circuits, and pileups of Russian thistles against the fences grounded out signals.

Costly long distance calls usually announced deaths, births, or very important events. One evening during World War II, a dreaded long distance call came to our farm from Uncle Dennis. He said, "We just got a telegram from the War Department. It says Billie died in France." I went to my cousin's funeral on my uncle's ranch to represent my family. It was the first time I ever heard an adult scream with grief.

While I was away at college for four years, I called home once near the end of my senior year.

My father answered the call. "DuPont in Port Arthur, Texas wants me to fly down for an engineering job interview. They will pay for the trip, but first I need to buy the air ticket. Can you loan me a hundred dollars? Later I can pay you back," I said. It was my first airplane trip. I flew on a noisy twin-engine Douglas DC3. What a thrill it was!

MAIL DELIVERY

Rural mail delivery service was outstanding as it was envisioned and established a century and a half earlier by Benjamin Franklin. The mailman delivered newspapers, packages, and letters daily to our mailbox by car except in times of heavy snow or impassible mud roads.

MEDICAL SERVICES

Adequate medical services were available through private practice doctors and a hospital run by tireless and dedicated Benedictine nuns. If hard-up patients could not pay their bills, the nuns accepted farm produce or canceled the bills. In exceptionally bad years, my father paid his hospital bills with bushels of fruit from our orchards.

OTHER RURAL SERVICES

Farmers still depended on pioneer traditions of self reliance for all other services. It was their responsibility to provide drinking water, sewage disposal, electricity, storm water drainage, animal control, care for the sick and elderly, libraries, parks, school transportation, school maintenance, flood control, and trash disposal.

♦

Many look back to times in the early and mid-twentieth century and think living in rural America was remote, dull, and harsh.

A young woman who lived on a remote ranch in northwest South Dakota expressed a different viewpoint in her diary. She and her three sisters made a summer vacation trip across the roadless prairie to the Black Hills—more than a hundred miles distant.

Her diary entries noted:

> Dolly went lame when she stepped in a prairie dog hole. A storm blew down our tent and spooked the horses. A wheel came off the buggy. Our water tank leaked, and we were sick a day because we drank from a livestock pond. Four rough-looking cowboys tried to get friendly with us; they high-tailed away when Margaret waved a shot gun in their direction. Fire ants got under our blankets one night and made sleeping impossible.

At the end of her diary entries, she summarized the trip:

> The brilliant, star-speckled night sky was a window into heaven. The natural wonders of the Black Hills were a sight to behold. My sisters and I may never again have such a marvelous time together.

CHAPTER THIRTEEN

THE NEIGHBORS

A good neighbor is a fellow who smiles at you over the back fence,
but doesn't climb over it.

—Arthur Baer

The neighborhood surrounding our bottomland farm was bounded by the Missouri River to the south, the Jim River (James River) to the east, the little town of Mission Hill to the north, and to the west the town of Yankton, the county seat and in earlier times the capitol of the vast Dakota Territory.

The neighbors' ancestral origins were Norway, Sweden, Denmark, Germany, Africa, Switzerland, Holland, France, Scotland, Ireland, Czechoslovakia, and England. They were mostly Protestants along with a few Catholics. The national origin, race, and religion of the neighbors were usually known, but it was never an issue.

Most farms were 160 acres or less. An exception was the Bob Yaggie farm; it was a section (640 acres—one square mile.)

My parents bought their rich, river-bottom 120 acre farm with its fine set of buildings and orchards in 1929 for $175 per acre. With the national economy about to crash a few months later, it was the worst possible timing.

Most of the neighbors were intelligent, well-informed, and progressive. A few, however, were "primitives." One believed a new radio tower caused the drought; he reasoned that it must be the cause because it stopped raining right after the broadcasting company built the tower.

**Neighbors Talking Things Over
on a Hot Day**

Most of the neighbors were socially active. Social functions centered at the one room Willowdale School on the corner of our farm: picnics, school plays, 4-H club meetings, elections, reunions, and occasional musical shows directed and produced by my brother Jack.

It was common for neighbors to visit each other on Sunday evenings to talk, joke, play cards, drink coffee, and eat cake. The visits were never planned; the visitors just showed up unannounced and were warmly welcomed.

THE SEMPLES

Bill and Edith Semple, lived on the fourth farm to the north, a legacy from Bill's parents. The fine Semple farm spoke of prosperity with its neat white buildings at the end of an arrow-straight, tree-lined driveway; a new Pontiac car; a new Model-B John Deere tractor; and a late-model Chevrolet truck. Most of the other neighbors still farmed with horses.

The Semples were always in high spirits. My father used any excuse to jokingly needle them when one of their favorite politicians—always the Republican candidate—lost an election or when they wrongly predicted the outcome of an affair of the day. The Semples poked fun at everything and laughed at every opportunity. They had the capacity to talk and joke with children as well as with adults, which endeared them to the children of our family.

When I was a teen-ager Bill hired me to paint a barn on another farm that he owned ten miles north. We provided compressed air by removing the spark plugs on two of his truck motor cylinders and using the compression to power the paint sprayer. If the compressed air and vaporized gasoline mixture had ignited we'd likely have been blown over the barn.

THE BECHENS

Louie and Mabel Bechen and their three children rented the next farm to the west. They lived in limited economic circumstances. They did not have a telephone; only a few neighbors did. One day Louie came skidding down our gravel driveway at high speed in his 1930 Model-A Ford, jumped out, and raced to our house to use our telephone. His horse was ill and in dire need of a vet. To a farmer living on the edge, the loss of a horse would have been a catastrophe.

Their tall, red haired son, Ray, was grammatically challenged as was typical of many in the neighborhood. Our teacher told him repeatedly to stop using certain ungrammatical idioms. Ray could not do it and the teacher, in exasperation, gave up. Ray later became well educated and abandoned his colloquial speech.

After a fall silo-filling job, my father bought a celebratory case of beer for the crew. Louie left for home high spirited and a little wobbly. Mabel read him the riot act because he drank so many beers.

The eldest Bechen son, Dean, was drafted in World War II. When he was discharged, he came home with a latent tropical disease that developed into a fatal fever. The entire neighborhood grieved at the terrible loss.

THE GRIPPS

Mr. and Mrs. Frank Gripp lived on the second place to the south. They barely existed in a tar-paper-covered shack on a small patch of land. Mr. Gripp tilled the land with hand tools. He grew vegetables and sold them from a roadside stand to earn a meager income.

When I was four, I rode to the Gripp home with my father in a farm wagon drawn by a team of horses. Mrs. Gripp had just baked a gingerbread cake. She gave me a piece to eat on the way home. The taste was strange to me. I did not like it, so when my father was not looking, I guiltily dropped the cake on the dirt road from the back of the wagon.

That evening my father said to my mother, "The table at the Gripps was set for a meal of only vegetables. I know they have no money at all so I gave them a dollar in advance and said I'd come back later for some lettuce when it was ripe." A dollar was hard to come by; it was four times what my parents could afford for their weekly church donation.

My mother loved animals. When Mr. Gripp walked to our house to do farm errands, he brought his dog, Ring. Mother said, "Ring is so intelligent. He understands every word I say to him."

Mr. Gripp always walked with a double-edged axe over his shoulder and Ring by his side as if he were the legendary lumberjack, Paul Bunyan with his axe and Babe his blue ox.

THE SICKMANS

The pioneer Sickman farm was the first farm south of our place. Joe and Louise Sickman lived there when I was a boy along with several of their relatives. Joe always wore the same outfit—blue bib overalls, a plaid flannel shirt, and high, lace-up boots. He folded his colorful wool stocking tops down over the top of his boots. Joe did not own a car. When he had business in Yankton, he walked three miles to town. My parents always gave him a lift when they saw him walking beside the road. Joe was a taciturn man; when he got out of the car, he invariably said, "Much obliged."

On a cold January day, Joe came to our house on an errand. When he came into our kitchen to get out of the cold, he broke ice cycles off his walrus mustache and tossed them into the kitchen sink. For some reason we were highly amused and talked of the incident for days.

Joe could not tell any of the six Lyons boys apart, so he called us all Pat, the name of my eldest brother.

Joe always spoke of my mother as "the missus." It was the rural habit to be respectful and formal around women.

Bill Remington, Joe's son-in-law, and his family lived with the Sickmans. While burning crop residue in the spring, Bill's six-year old son Billie caught fire and burned to death. My father quietly offered Bill a hand with the funeral cost. At the burial, Bill was inconsolable. "I want to go with Billie," he cried. He had to be restrained from jumping into the grave with his beloved Billie. My brother Pat was a pall bearer, a scary job for an eight-year-old boy. That evening at supper, our usual boisterous behavior was subdued.

Joe called on the telephone to inform my father that our hogs were out in his field. He did not bother to mention that they were running loose because he had burned down a wooden gate between our farms. When Joe communicated, he sometimes omitted information that was essential to fully understand his point.

A few years later, prosperity returned to the community. My father bought a car, his first new car. He and my brother Tommie were in the car driving the four miles from our farm to Yankton. Ahead of them was

Bill Remington driving his decrepit car at a low speed. Tommy urged my father to speed up and pass him. He would not do it. Tommie understood that my father thought it would be disrespectful and ostentatious to speed around Bill's limp-along car.

THE GIGGEES

Bernard Giggee and his family, who lived to the east, owned a small farm near the mouth of the Jim River where it enters the Missouri. He farmed with mules. His wife called him Giggee.

The willows and cottonwoods were always in a contest with him for the use of the rich sandy land. Bernard was a happy-go-lucky guy who was satisfied to just get by. He supplemented his farm income in the summer by fishing for catfish, bull heads, carp, and buffalo and trapping coyotes in the winter.

My brother Gene and I also ran trap lines for skunks, civet cats, and weasels. We earned the unheard of sum of fifty dollars for our furs one winter. There was a high demand for furs during World War II.

We acquired a large steel trap big enough for a coyote. We went to Bernard to seek his expert advice on coyote bait. He gave us a Mason jar of his customized bait; there never was known a fouler smelling substance. The cunning coyotes did not accommodate us by stepping on the trigger of our trap.

During the winter, Bernard let his hair grow long. Some said he had the brand inspector whack it off in spring. Brand inspectors owned shears that they used to cut hair on cattle to reveal their brands when investigating theft.

I once heard Bernard say to his dawdling mules, "Get along there you sobs." I was puzzled as to his meaning until a farmhand explained to me what S.O.B. meant.

Rural Saw Mill
Before Safety Guards

Bernard's brother Art farmed nearby. Art and his sons, Herman and Art Jr., had another way of subsidizing their farm income. They operated a saw mill using two Ford V-8 engines carefully synchronized to turn the forty-eight inch circular blade.

My father hired Art to fell cottonwood trees, haul logs, and saw lumber. Art would cut lumber to any specified dimension. We stacked green lumber in a drying shed for a year before using it. Cottonwood was suitable for framing buildings if it was not exposed to moisture. It was easy to drive nails into it until it aged. Then it would have been easier to pound them into granite.

At grain harvest time, Art earned further income by oiling and greasing the separator of Mark Welby's 1918 J.I. Case threshing rig. The rig threshed grain for all who lived in the neighborhood. Art was called the "separator man."

After dark on a fall evening, a couple of neighbors showed up at our farm. They said Herman Giggee had gone missing. They were concerned because Herman was despondent about Gertrude Brennan from across the road ending his amorous overtures. They shined their long flash lights up to the hay rail in the peak of our barn for fear that he had hung himself. Herman later came home after a cooling off-walk in the fields. This episode was big excitement to small boys.

After Art's wife died, he lived alone—he called it "batching." My father and I visited Art in his kitchen. His oilcloth covered table was arranged with a crescent in front of his chair with everything he needed for his meals: condiments, dishes, silverware, dry cereal, sugar, salt, toothpicks, jars of canned food, a coffee pot, and smoking materials. The dog's dish was on the floor beside his chair. I was impressed with the efficiency and practicality of his layout.

THE BLAKEYS

Three families of African Americans lived on small acreages west of us. Their names were Henry, Isaac, and Spencer Blakey—all brothers. They truck farmed and sold their garden produce in stands along the road. They also did odd jobs such as hauling wood and trash. Henry was distinguishable by his deep, raspy Louie Armstrong voice. The Blakeys settled in our community when their families were uprooted in Missouri after the Civil War.

Henry's son Teddy was our age. He had an excellent memory. He could recite the license number and owner of every car in the community.

Teddy remained in the area all of his life and achieved notable success as a business man, community leader, and head of the County Republican Party. My brother Pat, before the days of pussyfooting about political correctness, asked Teddy if he ever thought of moving to a larger city where he could socialize with more African Americans. Teddy said, "If I did that, I'd just be another black; here I am Mr. Blakey." Pat always invited Teddy to our family reunions as an honorary family member. Teddy entertained us by singing "Old Man River" in his wonderful bass voice.

Henry Blakey came to our farm to conduct business with my father. His elderly Chevy car radiator was spewing coolant and steam. He warned us in his hoarse vice, "Now don't put no water in my radiator, boys. It might bust my block." For some reason, only understandable to small boys, we thought this was a hilarious remark.

One of the neighbors said, "I can never tell Henry from Isaac."

"It's easy; Henry always calls tomatoes 'maters' (pronounced with a short "a")," his friend answered, "and Isaac calls them 'maters' (pronounced with a long "a.")"

They both called musk melons, "mush melons," as some of the farmer's market vendors still do today.

When I was a little boy I was in Sioux City on a street corner with my mother, when a group of black men walked by. "Oh, Mother," I said, "Look at those Blakeys."

In our home, it was forbidden to make disparaging remarks about anyone because of differences in race, color, gender, nationality, income, or religion. Consequently when the era of civil rights and women's rights came along, it took me a long time to "get" what the issue was all about. In my thinking everyone always had equal rights and deserved respect.

THE JAMESES

Orion and Lydia James lived on a small farm to the north. They operated a dairy herd with fifteen Holstein cows and one bull.

The James bull also serviced our milk cows. One of our boring chores was to lead our cows, when they were in heat, to the James pasture and wait for the bull to do his duty.

The James family car was a Model-T Ford sedan that was also the source of power for various farm machines such as a grain elevator and feed grinder. With the rear wheels jacked up off the ground, the tires ran against pulleys connected to the machine requiring power.

An artesian well with a four inch diameter flow of warm, mineral-rich water fed a pond dug into the sandy soil near the James house. What a place for Sunday afternoon swims and boyish mischief by my brothers and me and the two James brothers!

Mrs. James's father, Fred Dralle, lived on the farm with them. He mixed up a vile looking and smelling concoction that he sold around the county as hog medicine. He was a fixture driving on the dirt and gravel roads on sales and delivery calls while hauling gallon cans of his elixir in a two wheeled trailer towed behind his 1936 Chevrolet. Mr. Dralle always leaned back in his car seat with his chin tucked down on his chest when he drove. On Sunday mornings his car was sometimes seen abandoned in the road ditch, for reasons never fully explained.

THE SCHLAEFLIS

Bob and Ione Schlaefli, along with their big family, lived in a large house to the south of us near the sandy banks of the Missouri River among dense cottonwood tree thickets. Bob pretended to farm, but the source of his seemingly ample income was evident when he spoke of corn yields in terms of gallons per acre. In the thick maze of trees and meandering sloughs on Bob's farm, it was not as dry as envisioned by the enactors of the Volstead Act, the law that was supposed to end alcohol drinking in America. It was no more effective than if congress passed a law prohibiting drinking water or breathing air.

Bob was an adult version of Tom Sawyer; he lived his life as he wanted. He was a master of "the art of the deal." He bought anything he thought was under-priced. His farm yard was a parking lot for a fabric skinned bi-plane and a fleet of large second hand cars—Cadillacs, Lincolns, and Packards. When the cars retired from road service, they often continued life as chicken coops and tool storage sheds.

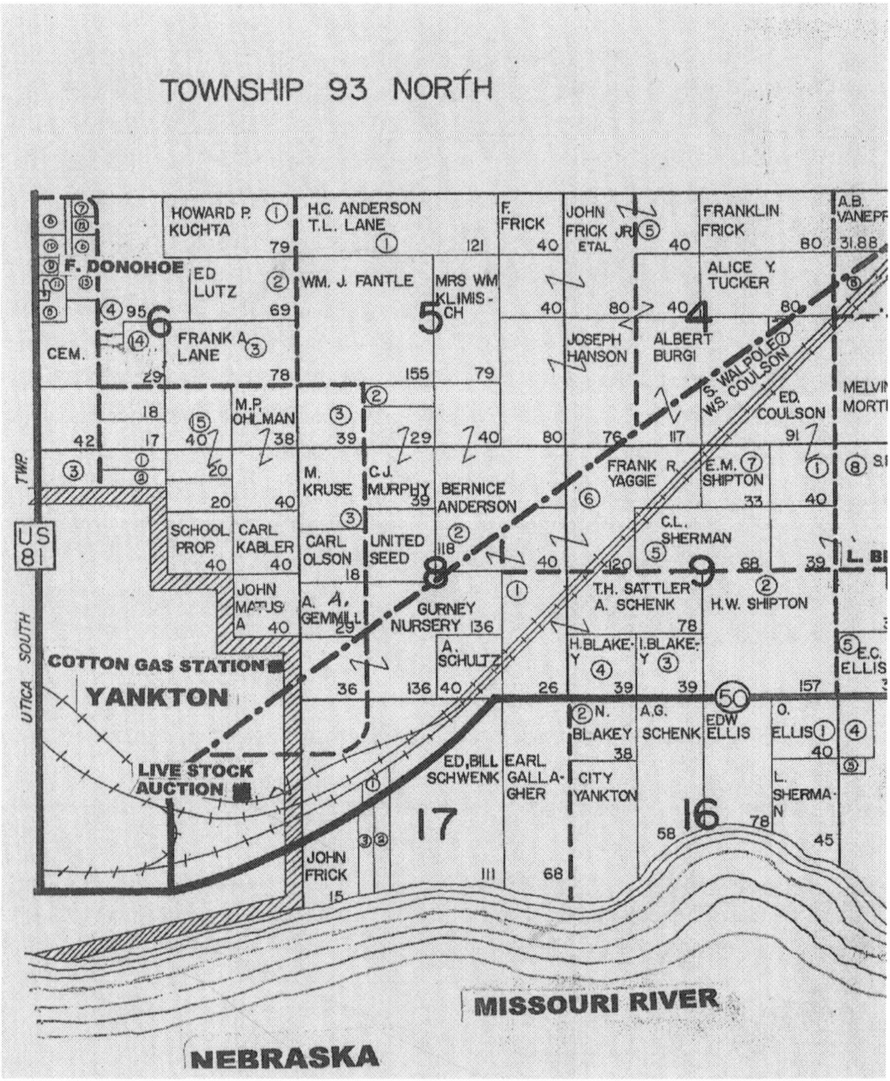

Neighborhood Map

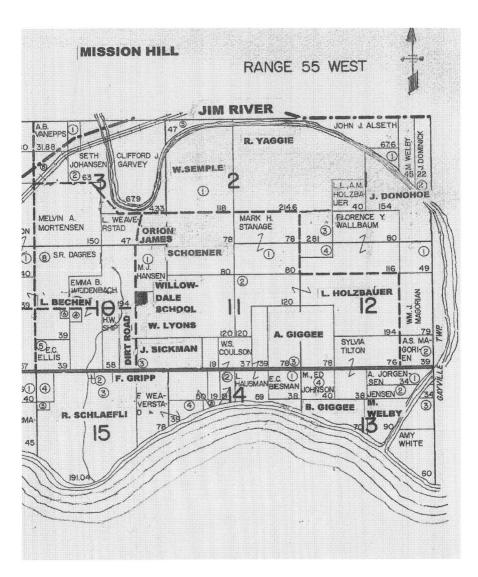

Neighborhood Map

Swimming Hole

A second-hand, self-propelled Massey Harris combine and an Oliver bulldozer decorated his farm yard but seldom ran.

Bob had a nose for locating and buying less-than-prime farms and woodlots. He had an equally good nose for knowing the optimum time to sell.

All of the school report cards for Yankton County are still intact in the courthouse. Bob's card shows that he attended Willowdale School for ten weeks in 1918. He was likely older than the teacher.

Bob owned a home in Texas where he wintered in a time when most people had not traveled out of Yankton County. He was always welcomed home in the spring when he arrived in one of his limousines with bags of fresh oranges as gifts for his favorite neighbors.

Bob never came to our farm without a funny observation or quip. He once came with his son Bennie and a small trailer of edible white beans. He wanted to use my father's hand-cranked fanning mill to clean the dirt and debris from the beans. There appeared to be a few brown beans mixed in the load. Bob said, "Bennie, throw them brown ones out; they ain't beans, them's rat turds."

Bob's son, Chuck, was my age. He and I delighted in "canon-balling" into the Missouri River by swinging out, buck naked, over the water while holding onto a thick wild grape vine suspended from a cottonwood tree limb—this in spite of the dire warnings from my parents that the river's treacherous eddy currents and whirlpools could drown us. We were lucky.

Telephone service in rural areas was on a party line system where ten subscribers shared the same line. When the line was in use, and Ione wanted to use it, she played her radio into the phone making it impossible to hear. A phone company representative threatened her with discontinuation of service if is she continued disrupting calls.

During World War II, Roddie Schlaefli, who could have been a matinee idol with his dashing good looks, jumped from a plane during training, his parachute failed to open. He was buried on a freezing, blustery March day. An army bugler tried to play taps, but every few notes his horn valves froze.

Burials are a formal thing; the grievers and friends came in their Sunday best. The older Lyons boys attended Roddie's burial. It took days for the neighborhood to shake off its infinite sadness.

At supper that night my mother, who loved poetry, recited the haunting words often associated with taps:

Day is done, gone the sun
From the lakes, from the hills, from the skies
All is well, safely rest;
God is nigh.

Years later Bob Schlaefli climbed down a ladder into a well in his farm yard to aid a grandson who had passed out from breathing muriatic acid fumes that he was using to clean a sand point. The deadly gas killed them both.

The neighbors always comforted in times of sorrow, celebrated in times of joy, and offered a hand in times of need.

Several of the next generation continued their lives in the neighborhood; others moved on to distant places. Some were successful and some struggled. But all forever carried with them the influence from the neighbors as surely as if they bore their DNA.

❖ ❖ ❖

CHAPTER FOURTEEN

THE THRESHING CREW

*Earth is here so kind; just tickle her with a hoe
and she laughs with a harvest*
—Douglas Jerrold

It was dinner time for the threshing crew at our South Dakota farm in the late-1930s. An iron washstand stood in the house yard outside the screened porch where an abundant dinner awaited. Each of the threshers bent over the wash basin to vigorously scrub his hands, arms, neck, and face while snorting to keep water out of his nose.

After the washers dried themselves on a cotton towel hanging from an arm on the washstand, they looked into the oval mirror over the stand and combed their hair—usually by running spread fingers through it. Some rearranged their comb-over hair from the sides to cover their milky-white bald spot. All were pale at the temples and above their cheek bones where their broad-brimmed straw hats shaded them from the searing summer sun. When they finished washing, they stood aside or sat on a long, oak bench in the shade of the north side of the house until everyone finished washing.

Each of the twelve to fifteen threshers, all from the neighborhood, wore a favored style of straw hat. My father wore a hat that appeared to be derived from a Panama hat design. Leonard Holzbauer's hat had a green celluloid section in the front part of the brim. Uncle Tom's hat was made of coarse straw in the style of an old-fashioned bee hive. Mark Welby actually wore a Panama hat. At the end the threshing season, some would celebrate by tossing their straw hats into the feeder of the threshing machine.

Some farmers hired men to work on threshing crews. Jimmie Donovan, a "raggedy-baggedy sort of fella," hired out his services along with his sway-backed team of elderly horses and a rickety hayrack. Jimmie's hayrack tongue was too short. When the horses pulled hard, the tongue slipped out of their neck yoke and made a tangle of his rig. Young Don Coulson sometimes sneaked in front of Jimmie's horses and spooked them to bedevil slow-witted Jimmie and his nervous team. Jimmie chased Don waving his pitchfork in the air.

Jimmie's personal hygiene habits were minimal even for a bachelor. I overheard my parents discussing where he would sleep when he came to our farm to work. A cot in the hay loft was ruled out for fear that he would complain to the neighbors that Bill and Mary Lyons abused their hired help. He slept in our house on a cot in a remote upstairs bedroom.

Teddy Cotton's Texaco gas station stood on the edge of shanty town on the east side of Yankton. His station was an informal hiring hall for unemployed men who were happy to find work that paid a dollar a day plus dinner and lunch. When my father offered a man a job others, who also desperately needed work, stood by.

Teddy sent Ben Holtz out to work on a threshing crew. Ben preached his version of the story of Jesus Christ during breaks while standing in the shade of a tree. The curious birds on their perches in the catalpa tree doubtfully cocked their heads as they listened to his fervent preaching.

The house yard cats disdainfully stared from far enough back to be out of the path of the basins of dirty water. Our dog Roly, a Collie/Shepard mixture, stayed closer; he liked to be sloshed with water. The chipped enamel wash basin was filled from a milk bucket with a dipper. The soft water came from the nearby cistern. The water had an oily, slippery feel because of its lack of minerals.

The tobacco chewers sipped a mouthful of water and swished it around their mouths before spitting it out along with a wad of saliva-soaked Copenhagen "snus" (snuff). The Copenhagen tins wore frayed round holes in their overalls pockets. Others took a last suck on their hand-rolled cigarettes and flicked the butts onto the ground before going

Dinner for Threshers

—Grant Wood

in for dinner. Most smokers carried their Bull Durham tobacco in a small cloth sack and cigarette papers in little packets. They lit their cigarettes by striking the phosphorous heads of sturdy wooden matches with their thumb nails. Adhesive for the cigarette paper was provided by a flick of the tongue tip. Seasoned smokers, including one-armed Clarence Cowman, could roll a cigarette with one hand.

The horses and mules had already been watered and were tied to the back of hayracks in the shade of the towering farm-yard cottonwood trees.

Non-controversial subjects were always safe for discussion during the dinner break: What makes a mule better than a horse—or a horse better than a mule? Will livestock prices go up? What is the yield of each farmer's oat, barley, and rye fields (the threshing machine counted and recorded bushels)? Where is the best place to catch catfish in the Jim and Missouri Rivers? And why can't Henry Wallace (Secretary of Agriculture from Iowa) and Franklin Roosevelt do more to help farmers through the depression with the emerging federal farm relief plans?

Non-controversial statements were acceptable at the table:

She's a goin' ta be a hot one again today. If it don't rain soon, the corn's goin' ta be a goner. I heard George German say on the WNAX farm show, the folks out west in Charles Mix County are butcherin' pigs and calves because the ain't got enough feed to keep 'em from starvin'.

Once in a while a couple of farmers would furtively duck into an open farm building door and whisper about a farmer's son "sparking" a girl who he hurriedly married. Soon she would deliver an eight pound "premature" baby.

Most of the threshing crew members who owned their farms lived all of their adult lives in the community. Those who rented farms, tended to move on after several years in the hope of a better life on another rented farm—few ever improved their situations.

When my mother or Leona Kast, our amply-padded hired girl, opened the screen door and waved a dish towel, dinner was ready. There were great platters and dishes of fried chicken or pork chops, mashed potatoes, green beans, corn, fresh strawberries, homemade bread and jam, pie, and coffee and lemonade. My mother, Leona, aunts, grandmother, and friends planned and worked for weeks to be ready for the threshers. Sumptuous dinners during threshing time were expected. If a meal was deemed inadequate, it would be "mentioned" later at the grain elevator, gas station, or farm implement store.

My mother was always addressed as Mrs. Lyons or spoken of as "the Missus." Coarse language was never used at the dinner table. It would be offensive to the womenfolk and children.

Mid-afternoon, the threshers took a break in the field and ate "lunch"—sandwiches, and hot coffee and lemonade. They sat on the car running board or in the shade of their hayracks.

It took one to two days to complete the threshing at each farm before moving on to the next site.

In early summer, Mark Welby, a neighbor, went to each community farm to find out who had grain to thresh and who wanted to be part of he crew that would go from farm to farm in July and early August to thresh the grain. Mark owned a 1918 J.I Case threshing machine and an

Threshing Rig Pulling into a Grain Field

enormous two-cylinder (two lung), steel-wheel tractor of the same make and vintage. Although his equipment was twenty years old, it looked and performed as well as the day it was manufactured in Racine, Wisconsin.

Mark bought his threshing rig from Bob Yaggie when Bob moved to Yankton, four miles away, to buy a grain elevator and feed business. Bob's farm was a section (640 acres)—four times as large as any other neighborhood farm.

The focal point of the tractor was its flyball governor—two three-inch-diameter cast-iron balls that rotated on a complex mechanism above the engine. As the balls moved in or out by centrifugal force, they controlled the kerosene flow to the engine according to the desired speed.

The threshing machine was powered by a flat pulley with an eight inch wide leather belt twisted top over bottom and running a distance of fifty feet. The pulley was made with a crown on its flat surface. The dynamics of this mysterious engineering kept the belt from coming off the pulley except when it broke.

Each farmer who signed on to be part of a crew had thirty to fifty acres of small grain—barley and oats and occasionally rye or wheat—to harvest. Before threshing time the grain was harvested with a binder, tied into bundles with hemp twine, and stacked in rows of shocks in the fields. Each crew member had a hayrack, a triple-box grain wagon, and a team of horses or mules for hauling grain bundles to the threshing machine and threshed grain to storage bins. If he had a larger field to thresh, he might bring along a hired man or son to work on the crew. Mark Welby was a farmer, so threshing his grain would also be part of the deal. But because he provided the threshing machine and tractor and he was a skillful organizer, he was paid cash for the use of his rig and planning the complex work of the crew.

Barley was an aggravating crop. It grew barbed beards at the end of each grain. The brittle beards broke into tiny pieces and irritated sweaty arms and necks.

It was a draw as to what work was the hardest on a threshing crew—pitching grain bundles onto hayracks and into the threshing machine or shoveling grain from wagons into bins. Both took stamina and strength.

My wide-eyed brothers and I were allowed to see the wondrous threshing machinery up close and to understand how the whole neighborhood was organized to work seamlessly together. It was an awesome experience. It was as exciting as the time a slow-moving steam locomotive made us stop at a crossing on our way to town. When the engineer, with his red neckerchief and striped cap, saw us waiting in our 1928 Dodge sedan, he waved and gave the eardrum-rupturing steam whistle a couple of extra toots.

Most farmers fed their grain to their own livestock—oats for horses and barley for hogs and chickens. If there was a surplus, they sold it to a neighbor or a grain elevator in town.

After the threshers—two at a time—pitched bundles of grain into the threshing machine, a rotating tined cylinder flailed the straw loose from the grain. Then it went through a series of shaking sieves and blowers.

Grain Shocks

The cleaned grain went via an elevator into waiting wagons and the straw blew into a high arc to a straw pile on the ground—all under the watchful eyes and hearing ears of Mark Welby. He stood—arms folded on his chest—in his Panama hat, red neckerchief, and immaculately clean striped bib overalls. He cocked his head like a dog watching and listening to his master for a signal that something might be amiss. On the rare occasions when his well-maintained threshing rig broke down, Mark took it as a personal affront. The crew knew enough to stay clear of him until he fixed the problem and his composure returned to normal.

The hemp twine that bound the grain bundles was chewed up in the threshing process and blown into the straw pile. The straw pile would be the source for animal bedding throughout the winter and an ideal place for growing squash the next spring.

Leonard Holzbauer let me climb onto his mule-drawn hayrack and use his three-tined pitch fork to toss a couple of bundles of grain into the threshing machine. He held me by my overalls suspenders to ensure that I did not fall into the machine. It made me feel like I was very big and

Grain Elevator on the Prairie

important. I hoped my brothers or other neighborhood boys would see me and envy me for doing such a big man's job.

Sometimes during the day, the wind changed and the threshing rig had to be repositioned so the straw would blow down-wind.

Mark Welby's special skill for maintaining and running a threshing rig put him in a similar position of esteem as the Mississippi River boat captains often described in the writings of Mark Twain. In the fall and winter, he further enhanced his reputation as a farm implement wizard by providing corn shelling service (separates corn kernels from cobs) around the neighborhood with his ancient 1918 Pierce Arrow truck and corn sheller mounted on the back The truck tires were of hard rubber and the rear wheels were powered with roller chains. The truck cab had a gracefully curved wooden top but no doors or windshield.

When threshing was over for the season, the crew was in an expansive mood. They prolonged the last dinner by telling stories:

> Mark Welby lived on the Jim River where he often fished. He told of hooking a fifty pound turtle. When he started to pull it into the boat he thought better of it, "If I pulled that big fella in, I might have had to get out—so I let him go."
>
> Bernard Giggee trapped for furs in the winter. He got the attention of the crew by offering, "I'll give you my secret recipe for coyote trap bait, but keep it to yourself."
>
> Bob Schlaefli quipped, "It rained at my place the other night, but it was pretty spotty. I forgot and left my double barrel shotgun standin' out against a box elder tree overnight after I was out shootin' squirrels. I'll be damned if one barrel wasn't full of rain water and the other bone dry the next morning."
>
> Young Art Giggee told of working on the Holzbauer farm where he had to pinch the ear of his red mule, Babe, with a pliers to divert his attention away from his kicking habit while being harnessed.

It was an occasion for the threshers to temporarily stop thinking about their hardships during the grinding, never-ending depression.

The end of the threshing season was a time to reflect on the warm sociability shared with neighbors. For my mother, who had poetry in her soul, it was a time to speak of the beauty and smell of the golden grain stubbles remaining in the fields after the grain harvest. It was a time to think about what would come next: perhaps a trip to the state fair; a dance in the GAR (Grand Army of the Republic) Hall in town on

Douglas Avenue—Lawrence Welk's Honolulu Fruit Gum Orchestra from WNAX (located just down the street) might be playing; preparation for the new school term and possibly of a new teacher at Willowdale School on the corner of our farm; taking 4-H club projects (cattle, hogs, and sheep for the boys and sewing and food projects for the girls) to the County Achievement Days fair; cutting corn to fill silos with silage in September; or corn picking after the first frost.

If there were not too many grasshoppers; if timely rains fell; if tornados, hail, and high winds stayed at bay; and if the grain harvest was bountiful, the community clergymen thanked the Lord for his blessings. However, if circumstances were less fortunate, they did not suggest that God should shoulder the blame; they beseeched him to help the farmers endure their hardship until next year when surely he would bestow better crop conditions. A few politically-oriented clergymen might divert the responsibility for crop misfortunes from God to officials in Washington— especially if the White House occupant and Congress were not of their favored political party.

In the 1950s, the fine social rituals and worthwhile work associated with threshing crews would end.

The combine merged the functions of the grain binder and threshing machine into one machine. After a hundred years of development and the improved rural prosperity following World War II, combines rolled across the endless, ripe grain fields of the U.S. and Canada like tank battalions crossing battlefields. An efficient combine could be operated by one farm family.

With the elimination of threshing rigs and grain threshing crews, a wonderful era of rural life ended. Many who left the farm to follow other paths would forever remember the excitement, good will, and human bonding that occurred during threshing seasons.

CHAPTER FIFTEEN

MY AUNTS

*Aunts have the advantage over parents; they can disclaim
nieces and nephews who don't suit them.*

My four aunts, two on my father's side and two on my mother's
side, were an integral part of my life and a significant influence on me
during my boyhood when I was growing up on a farm in the 1930s and
1940s.

ANN (ANNA) LYONS

Aunt Ann, my godmother, was born in Madison, Dakota Territory.
She was my father's older sister.

Ann worked as a teacher, an assistant county school superintendent,
a doctor's receptionist, and in a variety of public service jobs. She was
a responsible, caring person who sometimes had the air of anxiety
expected of a hen with newly-hatched chicks.

Ann helped bankroll my father and Uncle Jerry for tuition when
they went away to high school and college. Local schools seldom offered
education beyond eight grades.

When I was a boy of five, I visited Ann in Wagner, South Dakota—
sixty miles from our farm—for several weeks. While we were driving on a
country road, we saw a house on fire. In the middle of the road stood a
woman frantically waving a dishtowel to hail a passerby to help her
extinguish the fire. Ann said, "Oh Lord, that's Mrs. Hollenbeck." The
fire was too far along for anyone to help; the house burned to the
foundation. While Mrs. Hollenbeck stoically sobbed, Ann hugged and
comforted her as much as was possible.

My brother Pat was riding with Ann on a train near Wagner. She seemed to know everyone aboard. As the train slowed while approaching the depot of a tiny, remote town, a passenger observed Ann's gregarious behavior.

She whispered to her companion, "That woman knows and talks to everyone on the train. Well, I'll bet she won't know anyone in this little burg."

When the train stopped, Ann stepped out off for a few minutes. Standing on the platform was an Indian woman wrapped in a blanket. "Howdy, Ann," she said.

When Pat and I were about ten years old, Ann took us on a trip to the Black Hills in western South Dakota in her 1935 two-door Chevrolet. We went to visit my Aunt Mary who lived in Rapid City. It was hot, dry August weather. Sixty miles from the end of our four hundred mile trip, we stopped at The Wall Drug Store (a general store) at the edge of the Badlands for rest, water, and gas.

Ann had roped a crate of chickens on the fold-out luggage rack over her rear bumper. She opened the top of the wooden crate to water the parched chickens. This might have seemed an act of kindness except for the fact that they would be supper for a couple of weeks after we arrived at Aunt Mary's house.

My father had given Ann twenty dollars to pay our trip expenses. She placed the money in a white envelope and hid it under her car seat. A mechanic in the garage where she stopped to repair a broken speedometer cable moved it when he lifted out the seat. With her precision in always following the rules, she was afraid she might drive too fast and break the law. When Ann temporarily could not find the envelope, it seemed that the world ended until she found it tucked back in another location. Had it not been found, it would have been a serious loss. This was at a time when able men earned a dollar a day if they were lucky enough to have a job.

Ann lived for many years with her sister, Mary Robinson, in South Dakota, North Dakota, and Colorado while she worked at various jobs until she died.

Ann was a kind person. She is remembered in the community and family as the person of perpetual responsibility.

MARY (LYONS) ROBINSON

Aunt Mary was one year younger than my father. They were often thought to be twins. To be around Mary was to be perpetually entertained. Every thing she did or said had a humorous twist to it—especially to young boys.

Mary visited our farm home for several weeks at a time. Her personal modesty was nearly non-existent; while sitting in the outdoor toilet she left the door open so she could tell stories to us. She told a story about a family with a problem each evening blowing out the candle. Papa had a protruding lower jaw so he could only blow up. Mama had a protruding upper jaw so she could only blow down. Baby had normal jaws so he could blow straight ahead and extinguish the candle each night at bedtime. While telling the tale Mary dramatically distorted her face to demonstrate her story—a real tell-it-again story if you are four years old. It delighted us each time she retold it.

When I was four years old, at the end of one of Mary's visits, I hid behind the wood shed and cried. I could not imagine going on without her around to tell us wonderful, whacky stories and goofy jokes. How boring life would be.

Before Mary married, she periodically stayed with us on the farm to be near Vince Robinson; he worked on the power lines for Northwestern Public Service. This was at the time when power line workers had as much chance of a long life as crop duster pilots; the accident and death rates were appalling. When Vince breezed into our farm yard in his sporty Ford Model-A Roadster, we always knew there would be a rollicking good time with jokes, laughter, stories, and cheerfulness—and a little beer drinking.

Mary had nicknames such as Aunt Freak and Lucy Horse Feathers. Several years later when she and Uncle Vince operated a hotel and restaurant in Ellendale, North Dakota, my father addressed a telegram to "Lucy Horse Feathers, Ellendale, ND"; she received it.

When we were older, Aunt Mary lived in Denver and could always be depended on for a place of refuge for any visiting niece or nephew. While my brother Gene was earning his PhD in Colorado and enduring the intense pressure of his studies, she always soothed him with her Sunday night suppers and stories.

Material possessions meant little to Mary, which was a good thing because there were so few of them. To her, the treasures of life were good conversations, story telling, giving a helping hand, soothing others, and loving all who came into her orbit.

ELLA (ELLEN) M. DONOHOE

Aunt Ella was my mother's eldest sister. She left her parents' farm in Yankton County when she was a young woman to work as a stenographer in Minneapolis, Denver, and Chicago.

When we were children, Ella always had jokes to tell and funny gag-type gifts to give. At Christmas, she could be depended on to play Santa Claus and to clown around.

Ella, who was quite religious, often spoke of meeting Eugenio Pacelli in Chicago when he was Cardinal Secretary of State for the Vatican. Later during World War II, he became Pope Pius XII, the 262nd pope.

Ella once took my brothers and me to the Ringling Bothers and Barnum & Bailey circus when it came to town. The pageantry of the three ring circus was an indistinct blur, but I never forgot the glamorous exotic black limousine of the circus owner, John Ringling North, or the enormously long circus train loaded with animals and equipment. A promotion picture for the circus showed North with the swash-buckling Frank Buck. Buck was an "animal collector," movie actor, and author of a best-selling book, *Bring'em Back Alive*—the story of his exotic adventures capturing wild animals. It was all so exciting!

When I attended college, Ella always stuck a twenty dollar bill in my hand when I returned to school. Twenty bucks would buy two hundred "dimies" (ten cent glasses of draft beer) at the Silver Star Saloon in Rapid City where I was studying Mechanical Engineering at the South Dakota School of Mines.

Ella's parents—my grandparents—were for the most part enlightened people, but to quote my mother, "They had the Irish prejudices of the times." Ella had a boyfriend, Rob Welch, whom she loved and hoped to marry. He had red hair. Her parents thought people with red hair were possessed by the devil. They drove him away; Ella never forgave them.

When Ella retired, she returned to Yankton to live with her mother and her sister, Ann.

My thirteen year old brother, Bob, had a congenital leg ailment that required a two week out-patient visit to the Mayo Clinic in Rochester, Minnesota. Ella was his companion on the long train ride to Rochester and his stint at the clinic. They stayed in Mrs. Claire's boarding house where they slept together in one bed after they recited their evening prayers. Bob said she looked under the bed each night to see if a man was hiding there. It was not clear if it was a matter of security or of hope. She kept her larger folding bills contained in a small linen sack, pinned to her bra. Bob said, "Each morning she estimated her money needs for the day. Before she unpinned the bills for removal, she would say, 'Turn around, Bobbie, I'm going to the bank.'"

For Bob's first year of college, he attended Yankton College—directly across the street from grandmother's house. Each day he ate lunch with Grandma and Ella while engaging in entertaining conversation. During these times, Ella could occasionally be quite cranky with her mother as if she was getting even with her for the time she sent her red-headed boy friend packing.

When Ella died of cancer in 1956, she bequeathed her few thousand dollar estate to be divided among her thirteen nieces and nephews and to fund a small headstone on the family burial plot in the Sacred Heart Cemetery overlooking the Donohoe farmstead several hundred yards to the north.

It seemed that Ella's life should have been happier.

ANN (ANNA) ROSE DONOHOE

The Irish had only a limited list from which to select first names. Many on both sides of our family had the same first names (Ann, Mary, and Will.)

Aunt Ann was an intimate part of our lives. There was seldom a family weekend or holiday meal or picnic without her being at our farm. Although she participated in family affairs, it was always with a finely tuned sensitivity for respecting our privacy. It made little difference to her what the purpose was for a gathering; she just wanted to be a part of it. In some ways we thought of Ann as our second mother.

Many people could not tell Ann from my mother even though we could easily tell them apart.

Ann was well-educated with a teaching degree from the University of South Dakota supplemented by studies at Columbia University in New York. After teaching for several years in Minnesota and South Dakota, she bought the Yankton Gift Shop and competently and profitably operated it for many years. She specialized in selling china and glassware through wedding gift registrations. Her business seemed slightly exotic to us because of her regular buying trips to Chicago and other cities. This was at a time when many people had not traveled beyond the county line.

Ann located a supplier for nylon stockings—a scarce and valuable item—during the time of World War II rationing. She did a brisk business selling the stockings even though they did not fit her normal business model.

Ann traveled to distant places for her annual summer vacations—Alaska, Colorado, and New Mexico and in later years to Europe. She was often accompanied by her friends who were also single, professional women in Yankton. While at home they regularly met to joke, attend ball games, eat, and play cards. Later she often traveled with her relatives—my mother; sister, brother, aunts, nieces, and nephews.

Ann was always good for a laugh. She had an enormous capacity to poke fun at herself. She did not, however, indulge in any line of conversation that she considered undignified or improper. We all instinctively knew certain topics were beyond the pale for her. She followed a strict code of personal conduct without being stuffy, but she never told others how they should live and behave.

Ann took my brothers and me to see our first movie: *Snow White and the Seven Dwarfs*. For days we could speak of nothing else. We mimicked the queen by repeating her daily question to her Magic Mirror, "Who is the fairest of them all?"

During her many years in Yankton, Ann lived with her parents. After their deaths, she continued to live in their spacious house at 1103 Douglas Avenue. Ann was a pillar of family support, particularly to her mother, who lived to be more than a hundred. She provided tender and considerate care to her, either by herself or with the help of others when she was away for work or travel.

At a later time after my father died, Ann and my mother lived together for many years. They found a way to maintain their separate lives under the same roof, although where they overlapped there were occasional moments of ruffled feathers.

They shared the same staunch religious beliefs. A day rarely passed that they did not attend morning mass together.

Ann quietly opened her checkbook for the benefit of her nieces and nephews. She explained that if she held onto her money until her death, she could not share in the joy of seeing it spent. She liked to write generous checks to newlyweds with the string attached that they buy something they wanted rather than necessities.

When Ann died at ninety two, she made arrangements for the income from her modest estate to be paid to my mother for the remainder of her life and upon her death, to be distributed among her nieces and nephews.

The likes of Ann Donohoe will not come my way again.

♦

My aunts occupied a special place in my life. They were a lively and intelligent lot. Their parents—my grandparents—placed few gender-based

Ann Lyons
1889—1962

Mary (Lyons) Robinson
1901—1993

Ella Donohoe
1882—1956

Ann Donohoe
1892—1983

barriers in their way. Their daughters were given the same encouragement and educational opportunities as their sons according to the pioneering principles established a hundred years earlier by Emma Willard on the education of women. My grandparents respected their daughters and allowed them to make their own choices on which road to follow in life.

The positive and open roles played by my aunts seemed natural to me. In the 1970s when the women's liberation movement gained steam, I wondered what it was all about until I learned that many women at that time were denigrated and relegated to the second tier of life.

The women in my family functioned with few impediments imposed on them by the prevalent, male-dominated society. They at the same time played a nurturing role and provided a warmhearted refuge from the harsher realities of life.

Perhaps this point was best explained by Warren Buffet who is a genius at making profitable investments but profoundly unable to handle his personal life. For these needs, he depends totally on women: his aunts, sister, wife, daughter, and secretaries. Buffet, who could list his acceptable food choices on a speck of confetti, said "I'll eat asparagus before I give up women."

My life was better because my aunts were a part of it.

CHAPTER SIXTEEN

MY UNCLES

He's always come off like a nice uncle who knows things.
—Michael Musto

My eight uncles, five on my father's side and three on my mother's side, were a presence in my life during my boyhood when I was growing up on a farm in South Dakota.

DENNIS LYONS

When Uncle Dennis and his wife Bessie were newly married in 1909, they traveled a hundred miles west across the roadless prairie to Tripp County, South Dakota with all of their possessions in three horse-drawn wagons. They were moving to their just-purchased ranch with its cramped, wind-scoured house. They would raise seven children in the tiny house.

When one of the wagons tipped over while crossing a creek, Dennis dived in the water to find the cast iron lids for the kitchen stove. He never found all of them.

While waiting overnight to ferry the wagons across the Missouri River, a thief stole their provisions—a serious loss that had to be replenished with money from Dennis's lean purse.

During the dreadful Great Depression, fate dumped its full measure of misery on Dennis—grasshopper plague, drought, prairies fires, and crop failures. His land could only grow wind-tumbled Russian thistles and a few pitchforks of grass along Beaver Creek, which trickled through his ranch. It was not enough to keep his cattle and horses alive.

The most tangible products of the ranch during the drought were stone arrow heads and hide scrapers from the previous occupants of the land—the Sioux Indians. These artifacts were exposed when the sandy soil blew away. The Sioux were better stewards of the land than the whites; they did not plow up the native grasses that were well suited for holding on until adversities passed.

Dennis was seldom without his nose in a book—sometimes at the expense of working in the hay fields and tending his cattle. As a teenager, I presumptuously challenged Dennis on an item about the Civil War in a new Bruce Catton history book that I had just read. He said, "Oh, I have already read all of his books." I thought he was bluffing, but I soon learned that he had a deep knowledge of history. He also was a competent writer.

Dennis tended to be a curmudgeon—always ready to engage in pugnacious arguments. Nevertheless, he was a well-informed and an interesting conversationalist who could talk on many subjects. "Dennis missed his calling; he should have been a lawyer or a judge," was the observation of many who knew him.

He was a short man. He might have been characterized as a dyspeptic prairie dog wearing a white Stetson hat and boots while astride a quarter horse.

Dennis was a community leader for advancing soil and water conservation practices. He pioneered the formation of contours on his land to control water runoff and to conserve precious rainfall. When Dennis trucked his cattle to sell at the sprawling Sioux City livestock markets, he usually stopped overnight at our farm. My brother, Pat, and I slept together in a double bed. When Dennis came, we were often already asleep. In the morning, I sometimes awoke in the middle of our bed with Pat on one side and Dennis on the other.

Dennis was like the native prairie grasses; he defiantly hunkered down and made do until the drought ended, the grasshopper hordes vanished, the prairie fires subsided, the tornadoes blew out, and the economy improved.

JIM (JAMES) LYONS

Uncle Jim enlisted in the army before World War I to seek a wider view of the world and find a way to utilize his considerable intellect. As a private, his first assignment was to care for opinionated army mules at The Presidio in San Francisco.

His capabilities were soon recognized. After receiving his commission through competitive exams, he became a teacher of Military Science and Tactics at Drexel University in Philadelphia. During his long army career, he was also posted at Fort Davis in Panama, Fort Benning in Georgia, Schofield Barracks in Hawaii, and Fort George Wright in Washington. He commanded training units in Fort Bliss, Texas, and Camp Polk, Louisiana during World War II. He completed his career as a commander in occupied Japan.

While heading the Organized Reserve forces at Fort George Wright in Spokane, Jim commanded an Infantry Reserve officer named Harry Goldsworthy. Harry met and married Jim's beautiful daughter Edith. Jim coached Harry throughout his career until he eventually retired as a U.S. Air Force Lieutenant General.

Jim was a prankster while attending country school in Charles Mix County, South Dakota. When he saw a mule's head in front of an open window on the shady side of the school, he poked his Eberhardt Number 2 pencil in its ear; the surprised and frightened beast kicked the side of the school hard enough to break a window. The best way to make Jim behave in school was to give him a book to read.

Jim always maintained his roots in the soil of South Dakota. He scheduled annual visits to coincide with pheasant hunting season. His marksmanship was outstanding from having led a crack army shooting team.

To South Dakota farm boys, Jim was like a person from a distant world. He was urbane, articulate, courteous, observant, and smart. After his visits, my mother walked on air for days because of his silky-smooth compliments to her.

We were proud of him when he put on his immaculate army uniform with its epaulets, ribbons, decorations, and gold braids to come to our one-room school to talk of his experiences in the "exotic" places where he had been stationed.

After Jim became a Colonel, he always traveled with Corporal Hook, his faithful army issue "dog robber." Corporal Hook drove Jim's enormous Buick Roadmaster car, shined his shoes, pressed his clothes, loaded his shotgun, and saw him to bed—especially after an evening of whiskey sipping and story telling.

After Jim retired, he came to our farm for several weeks each year at corn harvest time. Even while wearing farm overalls and boots, he looked ready for a military parade inspection.

For years I penciled boyish letters to Jim. He always responded even though, during World War II, he had more urgent tasks at hand.

With Jim's courtly manners, he deserved to be called "Gentleman Jim."

JERRY (JERIMIAH) LYONS

Uncle Jerry escaped the poverty of rural South Dakota by attending the School of Dentistry at Creighton University in Omaha. His sister Mary spoke of my father and him running a grain header throughout their neighborhood at harvest time to earn money to pay part of Jerry's tuition. Jerry's older sister, Ann, also fed the kitty to help him through college. Jerry later passed on this tradition by helping a niece attend Creighton.

Jerry married Rose Gentleman and remained in Omaha where he practiced dentistry for the rest of his life. In the early days of Father Flanagan's Boys Town, he gave free dental care to the orphan boys.

Jerry and his family frequently were weekend visitors to our farm. They always arrived in a new Chevrolet sedan, a rarity in our neighborhood during the Great Depression.

Jerry was a dapper dresser in his well-pressed double breasted suits, starched white shirts, and in summer, a crisp Panama hat.

He and my father remained the same pals they were as boys when they grew up together in Charles Mix County. With their movie star good looks, they kept the eligible ladies of the county in a flutter.

Jerry's affable manner, ready smile, and easy going style endeared him to us. He made us believe our boyish interests and hobbies were as fascinating to him as they were to us.

TOM (THOMAS) LYONS

Uncle Tom, his wife Virginia, and family of seven children lived a hard-scrabble existence on the farm that Tom's parents lost during the Great Depression because they could not pay the mortgage. Tom later bought the farm from the Federal Land Bank's large inventory of repossessed farms.

When my grandparents owned the farm, they lived in a house made up of three homesteader's claim shanties pushed together. Tom replaced the shanties with a modest two story house.

As a young teenager, I worked two summers as a farmhand for Tom; I drove his combine, hauled grain, and built barbed wire fences around his fields.

He was generous about loaning me his car on Saturday nights so I could drive to dance halls around the county. As the "new boy" in the neighborhood, I was the object of much attention.

Tom had a tough time making ends meet. At the end of one harvest season, he did not pay my wages. He later sent a check for partial payment with a note about "hard times." My father asked me to return the uncashed check to Tom because of his financial difficulties.

At a later time, Tom's emphysema from years of smoking and breathing field dust forced him to stop farming. He moved to Denver and survived on odd jobs.

During most of Tom's life, his good luck rabbit's foot brought him mostly the bad luck of the rabbit.

BOB (ROBERT) LYONS

Uncle Bob, his wife Marion, and son lived on a farm near Wagner, South Dakota. His brother, Jerry, owned the farm.

Bob was the focus of attention for everyone in the community because of his affability and magnetic personality. He was the favorite uncle to a slew of nieces and nephews.

Nothing could be said that did not bring to Bob's mind a story, a joke, or a quip—especially when he was energized with bourbon whiskey; which he sometimes called "cow track water." The punch lines of his stories were anticlimactic; it was the story telling that counted.

When Bob married in 1934, his father gave him three dollars and a few coins for a wedding present. He said, "Bob, this is all I have."

He always looked like his lower lip was swollen because that is where he perpetually composted his wad of chewing tobacco. Standing downwind of Bob was not wise. The wheels of his tractor looked like they had been "brown washed" with tobacco juice.

Shortly after Bob's fiftieth birthday, he was elected to a seat in the South Dakota State House of Representatives where he successfully served for six years. He capped his political career when he was appointed to a vacant state senate seat.

His colorful statements during legislative sessions always hit the nail on the head. When there was a pending bill that would diminish milk purity standards, Bob opposed the bill. "Do you want us to go back to the old days when if a cat fell in a milk bucket you pulled it out by the tail and still bottled the milk to sell," he asked his opponent.

On another occasion Bob opposed the sale of a type of disposable diaper that he thought harmed the environment and was a nuisance if not properly disposed of. His opposition to the diapers started to receive notice in the national press. Two representatives of a major diaper company showed up in Pierre to meet with legislators and defend their product. Bob later explained what went on in the meeting: "These two slick city guys showed up wearing $1,000 suits and sporting $50 haircuts."

Dennis Lyons
1887—1891

Jim Lyons
1893—1974

Jerry Lyons
1893—1960

Tom Lyons
1905—1975

Bob Lyons
1909–1995

Until then few in South Dakota had ever paid more than $60 for a suit and $3 for a haircut. "When these dandies finished their pitch to prove the harmless nature of their diapers, I asked 'Sonny boy, have you ever tried to dig one of them suckers out of a combine sickle bar?'"

Bob measured the richness of his life in terms of friendships, public service, joyous living, tolerance, family participation, and a helping hand to all.

WILL (WILLIAM) DONOHOE

Uncle Will was a tall, slim man with a dark mustache. He farmed in Yankton County for a few years after he married Kitty Fitzgerald. He soon gave up farming and started a funeral parlor, first in the small town of Wagner and then in Yankton.

In order to attract both Irish and German clients he partnered with the Kabeisman brothers. To supplement the funeral business, they also operated a hardware and furniture store.

The mortuary was on the third floor of Will's home. Access was by an elevator built onto the rear of the house. The deceased were transported on their last ride to their graves in a stately, black Packard hearse. The grieving relatives rode in a long Nash sedan that also served as the family's personal car.

Will improved the odds that the families of the deceased would select the services of the Donohoe and Kabeisman Mortuary over its competitors; he was the Yankton County Coroner, an elected office.

Will seemed to me to be a remote man with an icy personality although others remember him in a warmer light.

In Irish families, untoward matters were seldom openly discussed in the presence of children; nevertheless, much was sensed. I sensed that Will was afflicted with the "the Irish curse." It was whispered that he "took the pledge" (to stop drinking) but only honored it within a short shelf life.

Will's life ended cruelly and sadly as cancer ate away at his tongue and mouth.

JACK (JOHN) DONOHOE

Uncle Jack, his wife, Helen, and daughter lived in Yankton. With his irreverent, salty humor and keen interest in each of us individually, we always liked to be in his company.

I loved to make things of wood. When I was eight years old, I made a birdhouse in the form of an airplane hangar and entered it in a contest. It won a blue ribbon. I received a telephone call from Ray Collins, a stranger, offering to buy my bird house for two dollars. At that time, two dollars would buy ten gallons of gasoline or eight "blue plate special" meals in Balfany's Diner. Of course I took him up on his unbelievable offer. Years later, I realized the buyer was Uncle Jack's crony who was set up to make his generous and surprising offer.

In the 1920s, Jack was an officer and part owner of The Farmers and Merchants Bank. After ten years of operation, the bank folded because it could not stem the onslaught of the collapsing national economy of the early 1930s.

Jack then ran The Cottonwood Packaging Co.—commonly called the box factory. The factory manufactured wooden egg cases and chicken crates. These products were in high demand during World War II because they could be stacked high in ship cargo holds. He employed seventy-five people divided into two crews; one worked in the woods cutting cottonwood logs and one in the factory.

Jack operated a boat, The RJB, on the Missouri River for hauling logs to the factory.

When I was a teenager, I worked in the box factory for thirty-five cents an hour. I removed cardboard egg separators from a machine and packaged them. The repetitive job was incredibly boring. It indelibly burned in my mind the need to get an education at any cost so I would never need to do such miserable work to earn a living.

Jack regularly visited our farm as he drove around the county buying logs—always in a new Nash coupe. He was fond of my parents. Many years later, I learned from a carefully hidden letter that he had bankrolled my financially-challenged father to buy my mother's diamond engagement ring. Until his marriage, my father worked to support his aging parents and younger brothers.

Jack also bought and built rental houses. He cared little about the appearance of the houses. They looked like they were built according to a plan made by his heel marks scratched in the dirt.

He was never without a tip on a low-cost stock or down-at-the-heals real estate. He was a bottom feeder who never paid too much for anything.

Most people of Jack's era experienced the crushing trauma of the Great Depression. Many became like Mark Twain's cat: because it once jumped onto a hot stove, it would never again go near a cold one either. But Jack brought the experience of the cat into better perspective, he took reasonable risks. His business judgments were usually sound and profitable.

Will Donohoe
1882—1973

Jack Donohoe
1887—1973

Francis Donohoe
1989—1948

When my father was dying of cancer many years later, Jack came to our farm and said, with tears in his eyes, "He's not going to make it, is he?" It was moving and sad for us to see tears from such a gruff, tough-minded guy.

FRANCIS DONOHOE

When Uncle Francis visited our farmhouse, he was always preceded by a gust of loud, infectious laughter followed by good natured banter.

After a university education, Francis taught school and served in the army during World War I before returning to Yankton County to run his parent's farm. He was somewhat of a "gentleman farmer" with much of the work done by hired hands.

After Francis married Ruth Moore, a college teacher, rather late in his life, he continued to farm. By then his parents had retired and moved to town.

When Francis and Ruth married, their raucous engagement party was held in our dining room. Francis opened some of the "engagement party presents." When he found a pair of lacey, pink lady's panties in a box, he wrapped them around his head like a turban. The next present was a water pistol. He sucked it full of beer and sprayed the other guests around the table, all to the sound of ear-splitting hooting and hollering.

Later in the party, my father spotted a hole in Francis' trousers. He found a corn cob and used it to plug the hole.

Sadly, Francis died of cancer leaving three young sons. After a few years of running the farm with hired hands, Ruth sold it and moved to town. She soldiered on and turned her Category 4 hurricane presence and personality to teaching at Mt. Marty College in Yankton while she ably raised and educated her sons.

◆

When I was young, I struggled with what career road I should follow. I liked faming, but I did not want it to be my career. I wondered if it was possible to launch a professional career from a remote South Dakota farm. Was an education from a country school and a small-town high school good enough? How would I fit into a non-rural community? Who could I turn to for advice?

When I realized that many of my uncles, from backgrounds similar to mine, had done well with their business and professional careers, I decided to look to them as my career role models. This realization gave me the confidence to choose a career and to commit myself to the disciplined study required to earn a college degree. And it made me understand that the only impediment in front of me was my own capability and tenacity. From then on, I sometimes struggled, but never doubted. Using my uncles as my career role models was one of the best decisions I ever made.

CHAPTER SEVENTEEN

WHERE THERE'S BOREDOM, THERE'S HOPE

And so, whate'er the weather,
He and I,
With our lives linked thus together,
Float and fly
…Touring upward, giddy-headed,
For the sky.

—James Whitcomb Riley

Author's note:

This chapter diverges from the authenticity of the previous stories and is written in the idiom of the community. It is based on a combination of facts, "inexactitudes," and fiction. Never-the-less, it all "could have happened" in Willowdale, the rural one-room country school that I attended in the 1930s and 1940s in Yankton County, South Dakota.

♦

It's so damn boring. There ain't nothin' to do. Louie ain't at school yet, and the Hogan boys stayed home to work on their old man's silo-fillin' crew. That means we can't play no ball today. There's so damn many Hogans that people call our school ball team "The Hogans." There's only nineteen kids in Cottonwood Grove School strung out over eight grades. We'd never have enough for a ball team if it weren't for the Hogans. I can tell ya one thing for sure though; we ain't never gonna ask no girls to play again. We was stupid enough to do it once. Lydia

Stonecipher made a dinky little hit and flopped around the bases like a gallopin' goose. Jeez!

Oh, boy! Here comes Louie now.

"Hey! Louie! What kind of a stupid idea ya got up yer sleeve today? I'm bored enough to try anything. I don't know what's worse: the baloney Miss Hanson spouts in class all day or my old man's dumb stories about how tough he had it in the old days and how that jackass Roosevelt's ruinin' the country. If I didn't have huntin' and fishin' to think about, I couldn't stand it no more. I can't wait to get the hell out of this lousy county and go someplace where somethin' excitin's happenin'."

"Billy, if ya'll stop yer jabberin' fer a minute and help me, I'll show ya what I come up with last night. It's gonna be a good one. Ya got a toad stabber on ya?"

"Yeah. I got one."

"Good. Go cut a willow branch about a yard long. Find one with five twigs stickin' off one end."

When I done it, Louie pulls his glove over the stick with a twig pokin' into each finger and the thumb hole

"Now what ya gonna do?"

"C'mon with me to the crapper, and I'll show ya."

Maybe Louie's gonna do somethin' as funny as the time he re-decorated Miss Hanson's Model-A Ford roadster. He turns the headlights backward and paints a pair of knockers on 'em. Then he pulls open the rumble seat lid and paints a bare butt on it. Ya coulda heard the ruckus it caused all the way to town. Drawing's the only school subject Louie gives a damn about.

We go into the boy's side of the crapper. There's only one outhouse with a wall separatin' the girls' side from the boys'.

Louie pinches his nostrils shut. "Damn. It stinks worse than a run-over skunk in here. Now, let's wait 'til a girl comes in the other side."

In a few minutes I whisper, "I hear someone comin' now. I think it's Lydia."

Louie waits until her clothes stop rustlin'. Then he pokes the stick with the glove down the toilet hole and under the dividing wall. He gives the stick a good flick with the thumb pointing up. We hear a bellow like a calf bein' branded. But Holy Gopher Guts, it's the voice of Miss Hanson.

Louie says, "Jeez! The crap's gonna hit the fan now."

The door on our side crashes open. When Miss Hansen grabs Louie, he lets loose of the stick with the glove, and it falls down into the stinkin' mess below. Then she grabs me, and I drop my old man's toad stabber down the other hole. Louie hisses, "Ya stupid idiot! Ya said it was Lydia!"

Miss Hanson marches us to the schoolhouse and pulls out the yard-long rubber hose she keeps under her desk. I ain't never seen her so mad before. Her face turns red and splotchy, and her hands are shakin'. "Bend over and grab your ankles! Louie, you're first."

She whacks his butt about ten times, and she don't spare the horses. Louie grits his teeth and grunts with each swing. When it's my turn, I squeal like a stuck pig, cuz I can't stand no pain.

On the way home from school, Louie keeps one hand in his pocket to keep it warm. "Jeez, I don't know how I'm gonna explain to my old lady why I have only one glove. They was a brand new pair too."

"And I know I'm gonna' catch holy hell from my old man when he wants his toad stabber back. He borrowed it to me cuz I told him I needed a knife for my school work."

After a while Louie lets loose with his hyena laugh. "Tomorrow I'm gonna throw that damn rubber hose down the crapper. Miss Hanson'll never whack anybody's butt with it again."

That night after supper my old man fills his pipe from his Prince Albert tobacco can. He lights up and blows smoke all over the kitchen. I stare at my feet until I get up enough courage to mumble, "I lost yer knife today."

He couldn't understand me, so my old lady pipes up, "Billy says he lost your knife."

"When in the name of God will you ever start to take some responsibility? You've lost darnn near every tool on the place." After he was through chewin' me out, he sent me to bed early. That was okay with me because I was startin' to get an asthma attack from breathin' his stinkin' pipe smoke.

I tear off my clothes to get out of the cold air in my bedroom. I lift Rex onto my bed cuz he's so old and arthritic. He crawls under the covers, and I put my arms around him. When the vet was at our farm last week lookin' at a sick mare, he took a look at Rex too. He said, "Rex has been a good, hard-working dog for a long time. But a lot of horses and cattle have kicked him and a lot of hogs have bitten him. I don't think he'll last much longer." I can't hardly stand to think of life without Rex.

I can still feel the welts on my butt where Miss Hanson belted me with the hose. I don't go to sleep for a long time. Dang it, hangin' around Louie and helpin' him with his tricks is more fun than listenin' to Jack Armstrong on the radio. But gettin' my butt whipped by Miss Hanson and chewed out by my old man makes me wonder if it's really worth it all. Jeez, it's awful to have to think about all of this crap.

I'm glad tomorrow's Friday so I can get away from the boredom at school for a whole weekend. But what'll I do after the chores is done? Maybe me and Louie can hunt pheasants for a while and then come back to the schoolyard and horse around. By then Louie'll have some crazy new trick worked out. Thank God we won't have Miss Hanson around to holler at us. She'll probably be parked down by the river in the back seat of Clarence Paxton's new Packard. His old man gave it to him when he got out of State College last spring. What a stupe he's gotta be to give a goof like "Packy the Puker" a new car. His buddies—he's only got a couple of 'em—call him that cuz after two beers, he pukes. Mr. Paxton's gotta be the richest guy in the county.

Jeez! I hate Mondays and thinkin' about another whole week in this crappy school. It wouldn't be so bad if Louie didn't have to stay home from school the next few days to help out on his old man's farm. He can't work none since a runaway sow knocked him over and twisted his knee. And Emil got drunk again Saturday night and fell through Pike's Poolroom window. Sheriff Brody throwed him in jail after he took a swing at him. Louie's mom'll probably bail him out this afternoon when she takes his dad to town to see the doctor.

He'll have a conniption fit when he has to let her drive the car. When it's muddy, she gets nervous and has a hard time holdin' it on the road. When they get home, Louie's old man'll probably tell Emil if he gets drunk again, he'll fire him and get a new hired man. He's threatened him a dozen times before, but it ain't never done no good.

I guess I'll try to amuse myself today by keepin' an eye on Floyd Grimes. Sometimes he does things idiotic enough for a good laugh. I don't know why Floyd even comes to school. He can't read no better than the first-graders. He flunked two or three grades. Now I reckon he's the oldest kid in school.

I wonder why Floyd's standin' over there by the school yard gate looking odd. Jeez! It looks like he's gonna' cut out and run across the road into the alfalfa field and high-tail it for home. I guess he can't stand the thought of another day of school. Floyd's in for a long walk home. His old man needed his horse today so he had to walk to school. Miss Hanson sees Floyd runnin' across the field and hops in her Model-A to chase him down. She's in a bad mood cuz dumb-ass Clarence wouldn't take her to a new Tyrone Power movie she wanted to see Saturday night. All he wants to do is park with her in his Packard and try to paw her over. God! He looks stupid with that greased-down hair and phony Clark Gable grin.

Miss Hanson catches up with Floyd over by the haystack when he runs out of breath. "Where do you think you're going, Mister? Take off your muddy boots and get in the rumble seat; we're going back to classes. And you're going to stay after school tonight. I'll leave the licking you're going to get to your pa after he reads the note I'm going to send to him."

Miss Hanson calms down after she hauls Floyd's ass back to school. Maybe shakin' him silly when she pulls him out of the rumble seat was like she was really doin' it to Clarence Paxton.

When dinner recess is over, I shuffle by Floyd's desk and whisper, "Ya stupid turd! If ya had the brains of a woodpecker, ya could've figured out she'd catch ya. Did ya really think ya could outrun her Model-A?"

"Yeah, Billie, an' you're a horse's ass! Ya better not get out of Miss Hanson's sight cuz when I get hold of ya, you're gonna look like ya was gnawed on by a pack of hungry coyotes."

"Yeah, in a pig's butt! Me and the Hogan boys stick together. If ya think ya can take us all on, go ahead and try. Your old man'll have to haul your black and blue carcass home in the back end of his wagon."

The Hogans almost never fight with anyone except each other. When the whole brotherhood swaggers up like an army platoon in Oshkosh overalls, it's enough to make most guys change their tune about wantin' to fight.

I pull a pulp detective magazine out of my bib overalls pocket. Lydia Stonecipher's ripe-dandelion hair cuts off the view so I think Miss Hanson can't see me. I start to read a story about a hotshot trial lawyer who argues in court with a smart-aleck detective while his bored blond girl friend chews gum and sits in the back of the room in her spike-heeled shoes and smears on cherry-red lipstick. When I come to the part of the story where the detective tells the jury that his dog learned more about the case from sniffin' the defendant's dirty laundry than the lawyer knows after weeks of studyin' his law books, Miss Hanson sees me and jerks the magazine away. "Billy! Why are you reading this magazine? I never want to see such trash in this school again. Here you are wasting your time when I know you haven't even looked at your history assignment yet."

I can't imagine why Miss Hanson thinks my magazine's any trashier than the stuff she does with Clarence Paxton in his parked Packard on weekends. Me and Louie snuck up on them one time and peeked in the back window. Jeez! Ya wouldn't believe what they was doin' to each other.

I'm so bored without my magazine that I doze off and tip forward. My head bumps Lydia's shoulder. She squawks like I goosed her. The whole class goes nuts. Jeez! When will I ever get away from this boring, damn school and these stupid idiots?

It gets dark when a rain storm blows up. Miss Hanson says, "We need more light in here. I'll sure be glad when the REA comes next year and we have electricity. I hate the nuisance and mess with these old kerosene lamps." When she stretches up to light the six lamps on the brackets along the walls, her panties show and me and Louie go nuts tryin' not to giggle.

At the end of the day Miss Hanson wriggles her finger at me and Louie. "I want to talk to you two after school." We stand in front of her desk. Jeez, I wonder what we done that she was gonna' chew us out for now.

She talks to us in that sweetie-pie voice she uses on Clarence Paxton. "If you boys would just pay attention to your studies and stop doing those dumb tricks that disrupt the whole school, you could be my star scholars. I know from your achievement test scores, you could get the best grades in the county. When you go to high school, you're going to have to study a lot harder than you do here at Cottonwood Grove School. You can do anything you want with your lives, but if you don't improve your smart-aleck attitudes and study harder, you'll end up breaking your backs on ditch-digging crews for the rest of your lives. And Sheriff Brody will be a lot harder on you for your dumb tricks than I am."

Jeez! I hate it when she calls us scholars like we was some kind of pansies. And I hate to think about goin' to high school and havin' to sit through four more years of boredom.

Stupid Louie pipes up, "That's good advice, Miss Hanson. I'll try to do better from now on."

When Miss Hanson turns around to dig her handkerchief out of her purse, I whisper to Louie, "You're fuller of crap than a courthouse pigeon."

Boy! I wonder why she smells so good; maybe it's the perfume she puts on her handkerchief or maybe it's just her.

Then she says, "And what do you have to say for yourself, Billy?"

Then I blurt out like some kind of dope, "Yeah, Miss Hanson, I feel the same way as Louie."

Jeez! I hate myself for that kind of sissy talk, but if I argue, we'll have to listen to her rattle on 'til the chickens go to roost.

By the time she lets us go, the rain's over. Me and Louie shuffle home kickin' our boots through every puddle and lobbin' stones at the green glass insulators on the telephone poles. Our aim's so lousy; we don't never hit a single one.

Louie slows down and says, "Ya know, I suppose Miss Hanson does make sense. I been thinkin' lately; we can't go on goofin' around like we do for the rest of our lives. I sure don't want to end up like Emil. He works all week, gets drunk on Saturday night, and is sick all day Sunday. Now, he's gettin' old and can't do much hard work no more. My old man would get rid of him, but he ain't got no other place to go."

"Yeah, I been thinkin' some about that stuff too, but I got too many other things on my mind. I can't do nothin' to make my old man and old lady happy no more. And it don't look good for poor Rex since he got old and sick. Ya know he's slept with me as far back as I can remember. And my two dumb girl cousins from Omaha are comin' to stay with us for a weekend. They go to some hoity-toity school for rich girls. My · uncle's got a pot full of money. I wonder what they'll say when they find out they gotta use an outhouse."

That night when I go to bed, I think more about what Louie said. One of these days I've got to get serious about what I'm gonna do with my life too. But my mind flies off in every direction like a flock of scared sparrows whenever I try to think it all through. I know one thing I've got to do pretty soon is quit followin' Louie around like I'm stuck to his butt with a suction cup. He ain't always gonna be with me.

Me and Louie sit on a cottonwood tree log in the schoolyard tryin' to think of somethin' interestin' to do. Louie's all out of amusin' ideas. He don't want to talk much lately until his voice stops changing. When he says somethin', he sounds like a cowboy yodeling.

We watch Floyd Grimes shut the school yard gate and turn his horse loose to graze on the weeds. Floyd rides his horse to school because he lives too far away to walk. He's nicer to his horse than most guys is to their girlfriends.

Floyd's dumb as dirt in school. He can barely read, but when he hears somethin', he understands and remembers it all—especially stuff about crops and livestock.

I punch Louie on his arm. "Hey! Look over there. Floyd's horse is going up on the school porch. I think he's gonna munch them leaves on that overhangin' tree branch. Holy crap! It looks like he's hunchin' up and archin' his tail to take a dump. Jeez! He's droppin' a pile of horse apples right in front of the door." We both laugh so hard we nearly roll off the log.

Louie finally stops laughin' enough to talk again. "Jeez, I think I peed in my pants. I don't think I'll ever see anything that funny again in my life. But let's not tell Miss Hanson. When she comes out to call us in from recess, maybe she'll step in it. And for God's sake, don't let Lydia see it, or sure-as-shootin', she'll tattle."

♦

Enough water has gone over the dam to fill an ocean in the half century since my days in Cottonwood Grove School.

As I sit at my desk in the office of the Secretary of Agriculture on Independence Avenue in Washington D.C. thinking about the old days, I decide to call Louie in Chicago as I've been doing off and on for years.

After my secretary explains her way through a couple layers of assistants at Louie's office, he comes on the line. "Hey, Louie this is Billie. How're you doing?

"Damn! It's good to hear your voice again, Billie. Things couldn't be better. What's up with you?"

"Pheasant hunting season opens in a couple of weeks at the old stomping grounds. How about taking a long weekend so we can do some hunting?"

"Great idea! When do you want to do it?"

"I'll check at the Hogan farm to see if any of the brothers are around so we can pick a date when they can hunt with us.

Cottonwood Grove School House

"When I bought my last farm, it had a pretty good set of buildings on it, so I remodeled the house for family visits. We can stay there when we hunt. After the old schoolhouse closed down, I bought it, along with the outhouse of course, and had them moved to my property. It brings back so many memories. I left the school house as-is except for new shingles.

"I'll call Floyd Grimes to set things up for us. I hired him to manage my farms when I moved to Washington to take this job. I depend on him to do things right. I think he knows every plant, animal, and square foot of soil on all five thousand acres.

"We used to think Floyd was dumb as a doorknob, but after he was diagnosed with dyslexia, we found he was actually smart as a whip except for his reading difficulties."

Louie, Rex, and Billie

Louie said, "Remember when we thought Lydia Stonecipher was such a dope? She went on and got a pretty good education. When Floyd married her, I guess it was about the best thing that ever happened to either of them.

"Our Gulfstream flies to our Washington branch office all the time. Shall I have it pick you up for the hunting trip?"

"Yeah, that'll be great, Louie. Thanks."

"Well, I'd guess with your hotshot job in Washington, things aren't as boring for you as they used to be at Cottonwood Grove."

"Yeah, that's sure the truth, but nothing since has ever been as much fun as the pranks we used to play. We thought we had the youthful right to misbehave, but we sure abused the privilege. I feel sorry for Miss

Hanson when I think of the grief we caused that poor woman. On the other hand, maybe we redeemed ourselves when we sent her that note pieced together from newspaper clippings telling her that Clarence Paxton was cheating on her. She dumped him right after that. She was too pretty and smart to waste herself on that guy."

Louie let loose with his familiar high-pitched laugh. He still sounds like he's as big a hyena as he did in the old days.

Louie said, "Recently, I was thinking about how bored you always were at school. I thought up an epitaph for you to consider for your tombstone: 'Where There's Boredom, There's Hope.' Of course you and I would probably be the only ones who'd know what it meant."

After we hung up, I stared at the framed picture on my bookcase of Louie and me in front of the old school house. We had impish looks on our freckled faces. Rex was squeezed between us with his grinning face and lolling tongue. We were confident that our knowledge of life and things within the mile radius surrounding Cottonwood Grove School was all we'd ever need to know for the rest of our lives.

CHAPTER EIGHTEEN

THE DAY THE DRAFT LETTER CAME

Back to the Army again, sergeant,
Back to the Army again:
Out o' the cold an' the rain, sergeant,
Out o' the cold an' the rain.

—Rudyard Kipling

A few years after my boyhood on our farm, I had my last tangible connection with the state of South Dakota. I stepped out onto the front porch of the house where I lived, along with two other engineering trainees, in Beloit, Wisconsin to pick up our mail. It was the summer of 1953. I was twenty-three years old.

When I read the return address on a letter to me from my home town draft board, a lump came into my throat. The dreaded letter opened with: Greetings, Your friends and neighbors have selected you for a two-year enlistment in the US Army.

Conscription was little changed since World War II when ten million men were inducted into military service.

The bloody three-year-old Korean War was still going on. Men were needed to fill the ranks.

My one year engineering training program at the Fairbanks Morse Company was completed. The company manufactured diesel engines, locomotives, pumps, electric motors, and iron castings in its sprawling Beloit, Wisconsin factory. I was eagerly planning for transferring to a permanent job in a new Fairbanks engine factory in Kansas City.

I had just bought a used 1949 Oldsmobile for $1,200—part of it paid for with a bank loan. I drove the car with the considerable pride associated with first car ownership.

It looked like the end was finally in sight for the Korean War—commonly called a police action—after the death of 37,000 US soldiers and more than 2 million others. Serious negotiations had been under way for two years with the objective of agreeing on a cease-fire. The war, fought since 1950 when communist North Korea invaded South Korea, was an affair of gamesmanship. Russia huffed and puffed and supported the Chinese and North Koreans but left the head butting to others.

A great global contest was underway to decide whether capitalism or communism would prevail throughout the world after the near apocalypse of World War II. Korea was not of strategic value to the US, but according to the prevailing domino theory, if any country fell under communist persuasion, others would also topple. An enormous pretense was made that the Korean War was being run by the United Nations. In reality the UN was manipulated by the US and NATO. At the beginning of the war, China crouched in the ditches in readiness, while waiting for marching orders from its Buddha-like Chairman Mao Tse-tung.

General Douglas McArthur, the self-proclaimed "Emperor of Japan" and Supreme Commander of US interests in Asia, believed his opinions should trump those of President Truman whom he called the temporary occupant in the Whitehouse.

He proclaimed that the Chinese would keep their vast ground army on the sidelines during the Korean War. The well-trained, well-equipped, and winterized Chinese army was of another mind, as it charged across the frozen Yalu River into South Korea with bugles blasting and bayonets thrusting. China still practiced the simple, but lethal, battle principles it learned from General Sun Tzu's treatise, *The Art of War* written in 600 BC. McArthur was caught with his pants down; the scale of the Korean War instantly escalated after the tragic slaying of thousands of American soldiers by the rampaging, bayoneting Chinese army.

President Truman, with the concurrence of the Joint Chiefs of Staff, fired General McArthur for insubordination. Under the new leadership of McArthur's successor, General Matthew Ridgeway, the spirit of the army quickly revived and the war stabilized.

During two years of negotiating to end the Korean War, the US could not make the compromises required for a conclusion; the negotiations were stalemated. US politicians would be fatally branded as "commie/pinkos" who were soft on communism if they made concessions.

General Dwight D. Eisenhower became president after his widely touted campaign promise: "I will go to Korea." His vast prestige allowed him to make politically acceptable compromises. The negotiations swiftly moved forward.

Although it was hard to understand the need for being drafted, I accepted my summons without protesting or weaseling for an exemption. Universal patriotism from World War II still prevailed.

After a short vacation on my parents' farm in South Dakota, I was inducted into the army at Fort Sheridan in Chicago.

Accepting an officer commission was an option, but it would have necessitated increasing my service commitment from two to three years. Because I wanted to return to the engineering profession as soon as possible, I took the enlisted man's option and started my "military career" as a buck private.

I worked at Fort Sheridan in Chicago for a month interviewing other inductees to determine their skills and education and where they would best fit into the Army.

I was assigned to the Scientific and Professional Personnel Program. This group placed technically educated draftees—engineers, chemists, physicists, biologists, geologists, architects, metallurgists, and mathematicians—into jobs that would utilize their knowledge.

I transferred to Camp Breckinridge, Kentucky for standard basic training under the jurisdiction of the battle-hardened 101st Airborne Division. The training was under semi-primitive conditions, but after living in the rural Midwest, this was not a challenge.

For the remainder of my enlistment, I was stationed at the Army Chemical Center in Edgewood, Maryland—a few miles north of Baltimore.

The mission of the Chemical Corps was to provide defense against chemical, biological, radiological, and nuclear warfare as well as retaliatory capabilities. Memories still lingered of the horrors of mustard gas warfare during World War I.

In later times, such devilish weaponry would be labeled "weapons of mass destruction." Fear of their misuse by irresponsible governments would become a permanent issue in the seats of power around the world.

Pinned to the uniforms of soldiers in the Chemical Corps was a pair of crossed chemical lab retorts. Considering the dreadfulness of the materials overseen by the Chemical Corps, it would have been more appropriate if a representation had been devised for the seventh ring of hell, as graphically described in the medieval writings and hideous drawings of Dante.

At the Chemical Center, I lived in a World War I vintage, two-story barrack with eighty other GIs. A coal-fired stove on each floor provided meager heat. The domain of each GI was a steel-framed cot, a foot locker, and a short rack for hanging uniforms. The layout seemed to have been inspired by farmer's hog confinement barns where each beast lives in a space just large enough to sustain its existence.

Our sleeping and eating functions, administration, and routine training were set up according to standard army operating procedures. First Sergeant Giannini from Northern New Jersey tried his best to accommodate our prima donna attitudes. In exasperation one Saturday morning when we were dismissive to his orders, he said, "Youse guys got all a dat education so why don't youse use some a dat s—t sometimes."

I was assigned as the only GI in a fifty person civil service office. My job, as a technical writer, was to create a maintenance parts manual for tank flame throwers. There was no urgency for the work. Our office was a "goof-off" place. The employees used it as a hang-out center for schmoozing, coffee drinking, romancing, conducting personal business (my civilian boss sold used cars while at work), and dozing. This was not

Barrack Living
(Room Service Not Available)

true, however, for many of my colleagues who had meaningful work assignments.

Because my work assignment was hollow and I did not like to be idle, I soon found other ways to use my time. Military posts have hobby shops for soldier's spare time recreation. The shops are equipped for wood work, leather work, electronics, photography, and ceramics. I was hired and paid extra to manage the shop and instruct GIs during evenings and weekends.

Upstairs over the hobby shop was an unoccupied mini-apartment. I surreptitiously lived in the apartment to avoid the inconveniences of barracks life.

After working hours, I used the hobby shop to design, build, and sell furniture and cabinetry and as a base for selling small power tools and lumber. I also took on house painting contracts. With the extra earnings to pay all of my personal expenses, I was able to bank my army pay ($100 per month.) I invested it in Westinghouse Electric Corporation stock.

I brought my car—commonly known as the "green machine"—to Edgewood. It gave me flexibility for sightseeing, dating, working, and socializing.

Soon after I came to the Chemical Center, the Korean War combatants signed an uneasy cease-fire; it was more like a formalized stalemate. More than fifty years later the "demilitarized zone" on the 38th parallel between North Korea and South Korea still bristles with mines, barbed wire, guns, and distrustful, glaring border guards.

The Department of Defense decided the cease-fire was not justification for discharging conscripted GIs. It is likely we were kept in service to counter-balance the threat of the enormous Russian Red Army.

But there was a good side to my time in Maryland. It was an opportunity to meet and understand a wide range of civilian and military people from different backgrounds. This helped me later in my professional career when work involved evaluating personnel.

Maryland and the east coast were all new and exciting to me with the Atlantic Ocean, harbors, big cities, history, and ethnic-food restaurants. Compared to the harsh winters of the Midwest, the Maryland climate seemed mild and balmy.

On several occasions, I visited New York City to spend weekends with my brother Gene who came down from Boston where he was stationed with the Coast Guard. During a visit to the UN building, we bought a souvenir crystal ashtray as a gift for our mother in South Dakota; few are the gifts that are too schmaltzy for doting mothers.

After a year in Maryland, I took a ten day furlough to visit my family in South Dakota. GIs were entitled to free flights on military planes. My barracks friend, Jim Endicott from Kansas, and I went to Washington DC to wait for a plane traveling west. After a day of futile waiting, we decided to take the next plane—no matter what its destination. We boarded a Navy Neptune plane bound for Jacksonville. FL. After a short wait, we found seats in the gunner's turrets of an Air Force bomber

Frank Lyons
Corporal US Army—1955

heading to Dallas. At high altitude the temperature was like the Dakotas in winter and the noise rivaled that of a forge shop. The cold, noise, turbulence, and my lifelong problem with seasickness made it the flight to hell. With no prospect for a flight north from Dallas to South Dakota, we hitchhiked on the ground for the rest of our trip. It was common for motorists to offer rides to men in uniform.

I had a barracks pal, Marcel Monier from Rhode Island. He dated and later married Jean Schramm, a young civilian biologist at the Chemical Center. She researched antidotes for deadly nerve gas-sometimes called Sarin or G-gas. I teased her about being "A Merchant of Death."

Marcel did not own a car; but if he had Jean set me up for dates with her college classmates, he could depend on me for transportation. Thirty-five years later Marcel and my wife Rita tragically died. Jean and I started seeing each other and in 1994 married. "Frank participated in both of my weddings—once as an usher and once as the groom," Jean explains.

While in the Army, I tested the life principles that I had absorbed in my childhood; they served me well. I also learned additional lessons that helped me for the rest of my life: friends may renege on debts; given reasons may differ from real reasons; enjoyment of life has little to do with money; acquaintances should be made quickly but it's best to make friends slowly; and deliberating before taking action may prevent ill will. And I learned there is tasty seafood (from the Chesapeake Bay) other than catfish and carp (from the Missouri River).

Because there was no active war underway during most of my enlistment and my duties were minimal, my fraternity-like life in the army was a lark; living was easy.

After two years of military service, I was honorably discharged from the army with the rank of Corporal and eagerly set off to a fulfilling engineering career in Moline, Illinois working for the John Deere Company.

FINAL THOUGHTS

The purpose of writing *South Dakota Days* was to recall and record events about the rural Midwest as I experienced them in the 1930s and 1940s. I tried to write in a way that would amuse as well as inform the readers-presumptuously assuming that there would be readers.

While writing, I retrieved memories of events that have been dormant for up to seven and a half decades. As I dusted them off, they became as vibrant and colorful as they were when they first happened.

Philosophers and poets have found many ways to say, "We are the sum of our experiences." The stories told in *South Dakota Days* are proof of this timeless wisdom.

My childhood neighbors showed me how a cooperative, tolerant community could harmoniously and productively live while surrounded by the adversities of the Great Depression.

My youthful experiences showed me that money, although it can make living easier, is not the most important thing in life.

The examples of my aunts, uncles, neighbors, and family showed me that all dreams are possible; the only limitations are self imposed.

My parents, who set "high expectations for success" for my six siblings and me, showed us that the only worthwhile life goal should be, "the best we could do."

I learned that if dreams could be envisioned, they could be followed. But the dreams have no bounds; I am still chasing the endless dreams.

ABOUT THE AUTHOR

FRANK LYONS understands rural Midwest life from his youth in the 1930s and 1940s on a South Dakota farm. After a long career as an engineering manager of a Fortune 500 company and the founder of an international consulting company, he turned to writing. He lives on the Mississippi River in Rock Island, Illinois where he continues to write.

Books by the same author:

WILLIAM and MARY
Their Lives and Times

THE DIE IS CAST
(A Novel about Corporate Corruption)

12909315R00091

Made in the USA
Lexington, KY
04 January 2012